MIGHTY WINDS AND GENTLE WHISPERS

THE PURPOSE AND POWER OF THE HOLY SPIRIT

BRUCE L. BLUMER

Mighty Winds and Gentle Whispers: The Purpose and Power of the Holy Spirit

The General Board of Higher Education and Ministry leads and serves The United Methodist Church in the recruitment, preparation, nurture, education, and support of Christian leaders—lay and clergy—for the work of making disciples of Jesus Christ for the transformation of the world. Its vision is that a new generation of Christian leaders will commit boldly to Jesus Christ and be characterized by intellectual excellence, moral integrity, spiritual courage, and holiness of heart and life. The General Board of Higher Education and Ministry of The United Methodist Church serves as an advocate for the intellectual life of the church. The Board's mission embodies the Wesleyan tradition of commitment to the education of laypersons and ordained persons by providing access to higher education for all persons.

Wesley's Foundery Books is named for the abandoned foundery that early followers of John Wesley transformed, which later became the cradle of London's Methodist movement.

Mighty Winds and Gentle Whispers: The Purpose and Power of the Holy Spirit

HIGHER EDUCATION & MINISTRY
General Board of Higher Education and Ministry
THE UNITED METHODIST CHURCH

To my father, Boyd,
who is my spiritual guide and
thought provoker.

To my wife, Sharon,
who is my patient editor and
loving partner.

To William and Nathalie Hyppolite,
who have shown me what
resilience looks like.

To Aaron, Jen, Dera, Beckett, and Ian,
who bring me joy.

CONTENTS

DISCOVERING THE HOLY SPIRIT

*But the Helper, the Holy Spirit, whom
the Father will send in My name, He will
teach you all things, and bring to your
remembrance all things that I said to you.*

—John 14:26, NKJV

If you've been part of a church, you can likely complete this phrase: "In the name of the Father and the Son and the . . . Holy Spirit." We're pretty familiar with God as the Father. We're pretty familiar with Jesus, God as the Son. But the Holy Spirit? Really, what is the Holy Spirit?

In this book, we're going to explore the mighty winds and the gentle whispers of the Holy Spirit. We're going to explore the purpose and the power of the Holy Spirit and discover the wonder of the Holy Spirit.

A couple of years ago, I came upon an advertisement that promoted an excursion to see waterfalls in the northeast corner of Minnesota. It was a beautiful drive. The highway borders Lake Superior, and there are many stops to see waterfalls along the way, so we asked another couple if they wanted to come along and share the adventure. What we didn't realize fully, however, was that there would be significant hiking involved. And that hiking would include unclear paths and rocky ledges, with significant drops and climbs to find some of those falls. The first waterfall we explored was advertised as a "1/10-mile hike," but it was actually a tenth of a mile *to the trail* and over a mile to get to the waterfall. But what surprised us most were these magnificent waterfalls themselves. The largest, along the Canadian border, measures 125 feet from the top to the rapids below. The falls all have different contours and cascades; each of the seven we visited was unique. They were beautiful, powerful, and awe inspiring. We went seeking waterfalls only to discover the wonder of creation.

In our lives, discovering wonder often comes as a surprise—we may not even know it exists until we open ourselves to the possibility. But sometimes:

- discovering wonder takes effort—a bit of difficulty increases its impact
- discovering wonder is significant—beautiful and breathtaking
- discovering wonder can come in different forms—from the noisy rush of water to the hushed sounds of wooded sanctuaries

Discovering wonder is also something to share with others. Together we're going to explore the Holy Spirit, a part of our triune God whom you may not even have known existed.

Hopefully you will find some surprises along the way, perhaps even the power of God available to you by simply looking. Some of this discovery may be difficult, but the effort will increase your understanding of God, and your faith, bringing you closer to God. My hope is that even though we may each discover the Holy Spirit in unique ways, we will all see the Spirit—with divine purpose and power—in new and beautiful ways.

══ Some Basics ══

First, some basics. The Father, Son, and Holy Spirit are collectively known as the Trinity. The Trinity is a way of describing how God relates to us and how we can experience the Father, the Son, and the Holy Spirit—God as Creator, God as Redeemer, and God as the Sustainer and Holy Comforter. You may also see the word *Godhead*, which is just another word for the Trinity. You may see *Holy Ghost*. This is the same as the Holy Spirit, just not used much anymore, as people have views of ghosts that may detract from our understanding of God. *Spirit*, *Spirit of truth*, *Spirit of God*, and *Spirit of the Lord* are all just names believers through the ages have used for the Holy Spirit.

We come to know God as Creator, who formed this vast and wonderful universe and all life. We come to know God in Jesus Christ, the clearest picture we have of the nature and character of God. If we want to know what God is like, we look at Jesus Christ. We come to know the presence and person of God with us and our entire world right now through the Holy Spirit. A modern affirmation of faith in the back of the *United Methodist Hymnal* says, "We believe in the Holy Spirit; as the divine presence in our lives, whereby we are kept in perpetual remembrance of the truth of Christ, and find strength and help in time of need" ("A Modern Affirmation," *United Methodist Hymnal*, 885).

While words are inadequate to capture the power and purposes of God, here is an analogy to help us understand how God can be three in one. H_2O exists in three forms: liquid (water), solid (ice), and gas (steam). Water, ice, and steam are three forms—three ways—H_2O is expressed. But who is the Holy Spirit? I think the Holy Spirit is the least known in our understanding of God despite some interesting books on the subject. Simon Ponsonby, author of *And the Lamb Wins*, wrote, "It has often been said that the Holy Spirit is the Cinderella of the God-head."[1] Robert Morris wrote *The God I Never Knew*, and Francis Chan challenges us with his book *Forgotten God: Reversing Our Tragic Neglect of the Holy Spirit*. Why has this part of the Trinity, with so much power and purpose, been forgotten and misunderstood? God is challenging us to discover this wonder, because we cannot know who God is otherwise.

Part of the problem is many churches don't preach or teach about the Spirit. My father was my pastor through my childhood. While he and my Sunday school teachers may attest that I simply wasn't paying attention, I can't remember any preaching or teaching on the Holy Spirit. It wasn't until earlier this year that the pastor at the church we're attending did a sermon series on the Holy Spirit. It was the first time I can remember hearing about the Spirit, and the Holy Spirit moved me to uncover more.

God's Wonderful Surprise for Us

The Holy Spirit will be a surprise for some of you—an aspect of God you might have heard about or perhaps you may not know existed. The person of the Holy Spirit is someone we need to look for and discover. We need to wake up to the Spirit's presence in our lives.

This might be your first surprise: you may have picked up that I've referred to the Holy Spirit as a *someone*. I think that's part of the problem: we haven't viewed the Spirit as a person. We have an image for Jesus, and many of us carry an image for God in our heads, but we seem to view the Spirit as a something, not a someone. I encourage you to start seeing the Holy Spirit as a person, as someone who dwells within us, someone we can connect to, and someone who is an empathic partner on our journey.

A. W. Tozer, in *How to Be Filled with the Holy Spirit,* stresses that the Holy Spirit is not mere enthusiasm but a person. He wrote, "Put that down in capital letters—that the Holy Spirit is not only a Being having another mode of existence but . . . is . . . a Person, with . . . qualities and powers of personality. . . . The Holy Spirit has will and intelligence and feelings and knowledge and sympathy and ability to love and see and think and hear and speak and desire the same as any person has."[2]

"There is an error that many make: they have attempted to understand the *work* and *power* of the Holy Spirit without first coming to know (the Spirit) as a *Person,*" wrote John Bevere in *The Holy Spirit: An Introduction.*[3]

Who Is the Holy Spirit?

My suspicion was that God as the Holy Spirit and the Holy Spirit as a person might be a new concept to many. To confirm this suspicion, I reached out by email and on social media with this simple question: What do you think of when you hear the term *Holy Spirit?*

I received more than two hundred responses, and while I am making some assumptions, I have grouped the responses in four main categories with the words that people shared:

1. Internal—softness, peace, intuition, inner strength, still small voice, calm, Comforter, conscience

2. Action—powerful, creative, presence, Binder, Unifier, energy, enlightenment, enthusiasm, mysterious, empowering, Encourager, wondrous, wisdom

3. Role—Helper, Counselor, Leader, Creator, Forgiver, Companion, Great Physician, Guide

4. Physical—Breath of God, a dove, dancing, fire, refreshing wind, renewing rains, teacher, goosebumps, violent wind, tongues of fire, gentle as a breeze, powerful as a tornado

The other word that was mentioned in the responses was the Hebrew word *ruach*, which means "breath," "wind," or "spirit." When used in reference to God, *ruach* in the Old Testament typically translates as "Spirit of God" or "Spirit of the Lord." In the New Testament the Hebrew *ruach* becomes the Greek *pneuma,* which is used for wind and Spirit, as in the Gospel of John, chapter 3. In addition, one of the limitations of the English language is it forces us to pick a gender. While *ruach* is a feminine noun, *spiritus* (Latin) is masculine, and *pneuma* is neither. A couple of the respondents found comfort in seeing the Holy Spirit as a feminine aspect of God.

Another interesting perspective put forth was that our concepts of God are shaped by where we grew up or live. This person referenced the book *Dakota: A Spiritual Geography* by Kathleen Norris, who believes our perceptions of God are directly shaped by the geography in which we live. Does the person who lives in the mountains have a different conceptualization of God and the Holy Spirit than someone who lives by the ocean? Than someone who lives in the jungle? Than someone who lives in a bustling metropolis? Than someone who was raised on the prairie?

As I suspected, there were few references to the Holy Spirit as a person. "The third person of the Trinity" and "the defining person of my soul" were the only direct references to characterizing the Spirit in the form of a person. As we discover the Spirit of the Lord, we look for internal prompts, actions in our lives, roles to assist us, and physical signs. Our challenge is to continue to see God as God, God as Jesus Christ, and God in the person of the Holy Spirit.

God's Footprint

In my seeing and discovering God, I have to admit that sometimes it has been easier to see God in the rearview mirror than it has been to see God through the windshield. For me, I have often recognized God's hands and imprints *after* the event, rather than seeing God as part of where I'm going.

My attention to the Holy Spirit over the past months has led to two big changes, and now I see God's footprint all over these changes. One is this book you are reading. As I've paid more attention, I have felt the power and purpose of the Holy Spirit despite my limited understanding of who or what the Holy Spirit is or how I have been impacted by the Holy Spirit. This book is an attempt to help us understand and grow together in our connection with the Spirit.

The other change has been how I respond. My encouragement for our lives is to listen for the Holy Spirit, hear the Holy Spirit, and then respond to the Holy Spirit. Throughout the book will be *Listen—Hear— Respond* stories to serve as models and examples of listening, hearing, and responding to the Spirit of God. Here's a personal example.

Listen—Hear—Respond

For much of my adult life, I've wrestled with a call to ministry. Being a preacher's kid (PK) and having several friends as pastors, I just couldn't see myself serving in a local church. Further, while I like to preach on occasion, I don't feel called to or capable of preaching every week. But I've always known that I wanted to be more directly involved in the faith journey of people's lives.

I was working for a national membership organization. While I enjoyed the people, and it is a laudable mission, it wasn't my "heart thing," and I was feeling unsettled. I was having lunch with a pastor friend, and we began talking about his part-time work as chaplain. He had been serving as a PRN (as needed) chaplain in a local hospital but was taking a pastoral appointment out of state and would be ending his work with the hospital. We had an interesting conversation about the chaplain ministry, but I wasn't sure it was for me. This guy is an adrenaline junkie. He served as a medic in the Navy and would continue doing chaplain work with the National Guard.

My friend introduced me to the director of the chaplaincy, and we began a dialogue. She gave me a book of "testimonies" from chaplains and asked me to think and pray about this ministry, and then we could have further conversations. Before the blink of a prayer, I was resigning from my job, starting an eleven-week clinical pastoral education course, and entering the life of a chaplain. What just happened?

Other events also led to this decision. Our financial planner is someone we truly admire for her intelligence, care, and encouragement to pursue our passions. In one of our sessions, she had asked me when I was planning on retiring. Honestly, I thought I'd work well past retirement age. She ran our numbers through a complex software program that provided an analysis to say we have a 95 percent chance of making it through retirement with the funds we have currently. I tell this to say, the availability of income opened options for me that I hadn't dreamed possible.

I must admit, I was quite naive entering the chaplain world. My first thought was, *Man, there are a lot of sick people here.* That fact probably occurred immediately to you, but I didn't and couldn't realize just how sick people can be until I walked in a chaplain's shoes. More than anything, I was surprised by the intensity of the interactions. I thought most of our work would be routine hospital room visits—"Hi. Nice flowers. Feeling better?"—but much of our time is spent with end-of-life issues, difficult transitions, and emergency or traumatic situations with patients, families, and staff.

At the end of the second week, I remember thinking that I'd been thrown into the deep end of the pool. I was involved with several deaths, including blessing a baby that didn't make it. My first and second overnights each included a Code Blue where the patient died. My experiences have also included being with families as they've decided to withdraw life support and spend their last minutes with a loved one during the death, along with some some difficult traumas in the emergency room.

But I've also learned from parents' deep faith despite the injury of a child; of the strength it takes to make a decision to move into hospice; how the dying teach their families, the staff, and me about dignity at the end; and the joy of recovery. I've observed the patience it takes to care for sick and ornery persons; the incredible faith that people have because of, and in spite of, their health condition; and that there are things worse than death.

What I've come to know is that chaplains don't spend much time in the kiddie pool. It's high dives, swimming laps alongside others, treading water, and occasionally pulling people out of the pool. It's made me aware that we're involved in very intimate and holy times in people's lives. God and others are teaching me to make the best of the small window of time we have with patients, families, and yes, hospital staff. Chaplains have to truly listen, caringly respond, and offer support as best as we are able. This ministry has given me the opportunity, despite my own limitations and fragilities, to be a conduit for God—Father, Son, and Holy Spirit. Being a chaplain has given me a front-row seat to experiencing the mighty power and healing whispers of God.

Just a few months ago, I was working in a full-time fundraising position and headed for retirement. Now I've started a consulting company and serve as a PRN chaplain. It all began by listening for the Holy Spirit; hearing the Holy Spirit through a friend, a director, and from gentle nudges and whispers; then responding to the Holy Spirit, taking a bold step, and making what turned out to be a rewarding decision to follow where God leads. What is God saying to you? Where is God leading? Are you listening?

Being Faithful to the Journey

As we discover the power and purpose of the Holy Spirit—as we work to listen, hear, and respond to the mighty winds and gentle whispers of the Holy Spirit—we find that the nature and character of God will always be far beyond our ability to comprehend. Our responsibility is to be faithful to the journey. Even when the path seems unclear, too long, or rocky, we remain steadfast. The reward for our effort is found in surprises, significance, encouragement, and a deeper, more satisfying relationship with God.

So we begin and remember these facts about the Holy Spirit:

1. The Holy Spirit is a person—not vague power or a thing. I am not saying that the Holy Spirit is human, only that the Holy Spirit possesses divine attributes, with which we can know and interact.

   "And I will ask the Father, and he will give you another advocate to help you and be with you forever—the Spirit of truth. The world cannot accept him because it neither sees him nor knows him. But you know him, for he lives with you and will be in you." (John 14:16-17, NIV)

2. The Holy Spirit is God—omnipotent, omnipresent, and omniscient—all-powerful, ever present, and all-knowing.

   Now the Lord is the Spirit, and where the Spirit of the Lord is, there is freedom. (2 Corinthians 3:17)

3. The Holy Spirit is eternal and holy. The Holy Spirit is not Casper the Friendly Ghost—neither flighty nor capricious—but is the Spirit of God who lives in us and among us, who goes before us and with us, and yet the Holy Spirit transcends us.

   How much more, then, will the blood of Christ, who through the eternal Spirit offered himself unblemished to God, cleanse our consciences from acts that lead to death, so that we may serve the living God! (Hebrews 9:14, NIV)

4. The Holy Spirit prays and intercedes for us.

   Likewise the Spirit helps us in our weakness. For we do not know what to pray for as we ought, but the Spirit himself intercedes for us with groanings too deep for words. And he who searches hearts knows what is the mind of the Spirit, because the Spirit intercedes for the saints according to the will of God. (Romans 8:26-27)

5. The Holy Spirit loves us. The Gospel of Luke quotes Jesus describing his message of salvation:

> "The Spirit of the Lord is upon me,
>   because he has anointed me
>   to bring good news to the poor.
> He has sent me to proclaim release to the captives
>   and recovery of sight to the blind,
>   to let the oppressed go free,
> to proclaim the year of the Lord's favor." (Luke 4:18-19, NRSV)

Conclusion

One of the things I adore about my granddaughter, and pray she holds on to for a long time, is how she loves everything. And I mean everything.

On an unusually frigid March day, she and I decided to go to the local St. Patrick's Day parade. Despite our efforts, no one else in the family wanted to join us. It was cold, and we huddled on the curb to stay warm. The parade started late and was sketchy at best. Many of the participants had a "wee bit" before the parade, and I was second-guessing this adventure. After the parade I asked my granddaughter what she thought, and she said, "This is the best parade I've ever been to."

Over the holidays, the city near where we live transforms a park into a winter wonderland. There are lights and lighted decorations on most of the trees and buildings, and the park highlights the waterfalls with vibrant-colored floodlights. It was great to see this through the eyes of my granddaughter. We drove through the park slowly, and she was taking it all in, but insisted we get out of the car and walk to see the lights more closely. When we got out of the car, you could hear the Christmas music.

"Papa, the trees are singing." *They sure are.*

"The water is so beautiful. How do they make the colors?" *I pointed out the floodlights that illuminate the falls.*

"It would take a lot of people to take these lights down." *Yep, it sure would.*

"How do they get lights on the tall trees?" *We decided a big ladder or a truck with a bucket.*

"Let's walk across the bridge to the other side." *Even though we were both shivering, she just couldn't stop.*

After another look at the water, we got back into the car, and as we were leaving the park, she saw the large Catholic cathedral.

"Can we go see it?" *Sure!*

"Is that a castle? Who lives in that castle?" *Well, it's a church, so people don't live in there.*

"Do you think angels live up there?" *Where?*

"Way up in the top by those lights." *There probably are. Those spires are over 180 feet tall.*

The word that came to me was *awe*. Thousands of lights, colorful waterfalls, singing trees, and a castle with angels—these created awe for my granddaughter. Ah, the eyes of a child—open to wonder, eager to experience the goodness of life. Be in awe of nature and things of the world. Be in awe of the gifts we have been given. Be in awe of simple things—even stumbling, silly persons. Be in awe for how much this little girl can teach me. Let's be in awe of God as God, God as Jesus, and God as the Holy Spirit.

We set aside our fears, assumptions, and preconceived notions. We accept an openness to learn more. We allow the Holy Spirit to dwell within us, connect with us, and serve as a faithful guide on our journey.

═══ Let Us Pray ═══

There is a lovely song titled "Holy Spirit" recorded by Francesca Battistelli and written by Katie Torwalt and Bryan Wilson. Let its last lines be our prayer: *"Let us become more aware of Your presence. Let us experience the glory of Your goodness." Amen.*[4]

═══ Reflection Questions ═══

1. What was your biggest takeaway from the chapter?

2. Think of a time when you discovered a place or something or someone. Was there a surprise? Did it take effort? Do you see it differently now? How has the discovery become significant for you? How have you been able to share it with others?

3. How would you tell another person about the Trinity? The Holy Spirit?

4. Do you have an example of when you looked in the "rearview mirror" and realized God was completely a part of that experience?

5. When was the last time you listened for, heard, and responded to the Holy Spirit?

WINDS AND WHISPERS OF THE HOLY SPIRIT THROUGH SCRIPTURE

Once people have seen the light, gotten a taste of heaven and been part of the work of the Holy Spirit, once they've personally experienced the sheer goodness of God's Word and the powers breaking in on us—if then they turn their backs on it, washing their hands of the whole thing, well, they can't start over as if nothing happened. That's impossible.

—Hebrews 6:4-6, *The Message*

As we begin this discovery of the Holy Spirit, Scripture seems like a good place to start. Let's use the Bible as a road map for our journey. The Bible begins this way:

> In the beginning God created the heavens and the earth. Now the earth was formless and empty, darkness was over the surface of the deep, and the Spirit of God was hovering over the waters. (Genesis 1:1-2, NIV)

The Hovering Spirit

The first thing the Bible does is tell us that God created everything. The second thing it does is introduce us to the Holy Spirit. I'm pretty sure that since the Spirit of God is in the second sentence of *the entire Bible*, it's a big deal. Up front the Bible lets us know that God is a creating God and that God requires nothing to create—everything was created out of nothing—God speaks and creation happens. That incomprehensible act was initiated and accomplished by God, who made all that is, including this beautiful earth, from emptiness and darkness.

An integral part of creation was the Holy Spirit. The Spirit hovering over the waters has been compared to a bird incubating or brooding over eggs. What does the third verse of Genesis say? "And God said, 'Let there be light,' and there was light." The Spirit of God began by "hatching" light. There was nothing—all was formless, empty, and dark—and then, light! And creation begins and culminates with goodness and beauty by the power of the Holy Spirit. The Spirit was present and working from the very beginning.

The Holy Spirit also brings light into our lives, hovering over our darkness and emptiness and waiting for that first crack, to bring us light. We have the opportunity to discover and then attach to the power that God wants to create for each of us.

The Holy Spirit is not meant to be a secret. Rather, we see the Holy Spirit acting throughout Genesis and then in references throughout the entire Bible. The Holy Spirit is mentioned more than ninety times, the Spirit of the Lord more than twenty-five times, and the Spirit of God more than twenty-five times in the Bible. The Scriptures are inviting us and connecting us to the winds and whispers of the Holy Spirit.

Listen—Hear—Respond

T. B. S. tells it this way:

Part of my role in Welcoming Ministries at my church is to connect people. Maybe people need to find childcare, a Sunday school class, a small group, a helping ministry, and at times a pastor. Sometimes I feel that I am the help desk, there to receive and deliver messages.

One Sunday, I was greeting a woman new to our church, and I was trying to make her feel welcome. After the service, she came to thank me but also to share that she had had a strong sense that she needed to be at church this morning to hear the pastor's sermon. Then she broke down. She had lost her husband only two weeks ago, and later I found out it was because of suicide.

I introduced her to one of our pastors, who listened and comforted her, and then made a connection to the woman's pastor in her hometown. People who offer the ministry of welcome and hospitality have opportunities to link the Holy Spirit to the right people at the right time. It is also about responding—the woman responding to us and us responding to her.

Several months later I had a vivid dream that woke me up, and I can still visualize it to this day. I thought I was having a medical incident; I was flushed, and my heart was beating so fast. The feelings gave me the definite and powerful message that something big was going to happen but that it was going to be okay. And that God is good. I replayed this message over and over in my mind and couldn't figure out what it meant. Was it for my life? Was it for our church? A few hours later I got another powerful message that I needed to tell my lead pastor. Once I made the call and offered the message, I finally felt at peace.

I found out later that when I was talking to the lead pastor, the pastor had just been asked to serve at another church but was struggling with the impact on their family. It was comforting to our pastor and comforting for me that I was able to be the conduit for a message of the Holy Spirit.

The Spirit of God comes as whispers, thoughts, dreams, and many other forms. It is our obligation to be attentive to the gentle whispers, because it is our attentiveness, our attunement with God, that makes all the difference and opens us to receiving God's grace. Robert Morris, in *The God I Never Knew*, tells us:

> So you're not likely to hear an audible voice. Instead it comes as a *thought*. So it's easy to question whether the message is your own or something the Spirit is telling you.
>
> With time and familiarity, however, you can learn to clearly distinguish between thoughts that are your own and those that come from the Spirit. . . . The more you hear, recognize, and acknowledge [God's] voice, the easier it will be to hear [God] every time [God] speaks.[5]

Again, our role is to listen, hear, and then respond to the Spirit. Whispers are one way, but there have been times that the Holy Spirit also came with the roar of a mighty wind or in more dramatic ways. We will examine two books of the Bible—Acts and John—to show the winds of the Holy Spirit.

The book of Acts has been called the Gospel of the Holy Spirit and is a good place to be introduced to the power and influence of the Spirit. In Acts, there are forty references to the Holy Spirit in just the first thirteen chapters. Also called the Acts of the Apostles, this book highlights how the Spirit came to the early Christian church in a special way, during a Jewish festival called the day of Pentecost. However, "it is perhaps unfortunate that we speak of the events at Pentecost as the coming of the Holy Spirit. The danger is that we may think that the Holy Spirit came into existence at that time," stated William Barclay in *Daily Study Bible.*[6] We know that the Spirit was part of God's impact from the beginning, but this was a special and important revealing of God and God's power to God's people.

Pentecost is one of three great Jewish festivals, and persons who lived within twenty miles of Jerusalem would have been legally bound to attend. But Jews from around the world attended, so Jerusalem was filled to overflowing. Not only would there be a great gathering of people; they would be "from every nation under heaven" (Acts 2:5). Acts 2, starting in verse 8, lists some of these places, with each speaking in their own language—quite the diverse and international crowd.

The festival's historical significance was the commemoration of Moses receiving the Law on Mount Sinai. In addition, there was agricultural significance to Pentecost, also called the day of first fruits, because there was an offering of the first barley crop to God. The first loaves made with the new grain crop would have been placed on the altar and offered as a thanksgiving to God.

With Pentecost as the backdrop, the early church was just getting organized and off the ground. These believers in the way of Jesus had no official name and considered themselves Jews. They sought the Holy Spirit as the source of their guidance. The leaders were persons who connected with the Spirit of God. In Acts 1:14, they were gathered and were praying "with one accord." Luke, the writer of Acts, wanted to demonstrate that Jesus came for all people, regardless of gender, religion, social status, age, race, or creed. In some measure, this is one reason Christianity became a worldwide religion. It was available to all. Jesus's salvation extended to everyone. It was available to this diverse crowd. God used Pentecost as a great opportunity to connect and expand the circle of Jesus's followers. And here is where the Holy Spirit enters the picture.

In Acts 2:1-4 we read:

> When the Day of Pentecost had fully come, they were all with one accord in one place. And suddenly there came a sound from heaven, as of a rushing mighty wind, and it filled the whole house where they were sitting. Then there appeared to them divided tongues, as of fire, and one sat upon each of them. And they were all filled with the Holy Spirit and began to speak with other tongues, as the Spirit gave them utterance. (NKJV)

The 120 core followers of Jesus, including the eleven disciples, were "in one place" and "with one accord." Imagine a church meeting where everyone came, got along, and was happy with the lunch. These apostles would have experienced the rushing wind, tongues of fire, and speaking in other languages. Most important, they were all filled with the Holy Spirit.

Think of how confirming this would have been for the leaders. How it galvanized their resolve to tell others about Jesus, about God, and about the power of the Holy Spirit. The followers of Jesus listened, heard, and responded. No wonder Peter could proclaim a message and move a crowd to join their ranks (Acts 2:41).

One of the most controversial aspects related to Acts 2 is the speaking in tongues. We will take this up in more depth later in the book, and my point is not to divide or defend. My point is to highlight that people experience the Spirit in powerful ways. Throughout this book, my theme will be that we experience God in different ways and that our experiences shouldn't define or limit another person's experience. Our role is to seek the Spirit in all things.

With all of this as a background, William Barclay provides this perspective:

> What happened at Pentecost we really do not know. Certain it is that the disciples had an experience of the power of the Spirit flooding their beings such as they never had before. We must remember that for this part of Acts, Luke (the author of Acts) was not an eyewitness and that he was passing on a story which he must have heard. He tells the story as if the disciples suddenly acquired the gift of speaking in *foreign* languages. For two reasons that is not likely. . . . There was in the early Church a phenomenon which has never completely passed away. It was called *speaking with tongues*. What happened was someone, in an ecstasy, began to pour out a flood of unintelligible sounds in no known language. This was supposed to be directly inspired by the Spirit of God. Strange as it sounds, it was greatly coveted. Paul did not greatly approve of it, because it seemed to him far to be preferred that a message should be in a language that could be understood.
>
> It seems by far most likely that Luke, a Gentile, had confused speaking with tongues with speaking with *foreign* tongues.[7]

Regardless, the group received a clear and powerful message that could be shared and could reach the hearts of others. So powerful is that following Peter's message, three thousand people were baptized and committed themselves to Jesus Christ. No longer bound by fear and failure, Peter was now free to respond, and he did so with the first Christian sermon ever preached.

Such was the situation facing Peter on the Day of Pentecost. The sound of the rushing wind from heaven had drawn a large crowd, which then heard all the believers speaking of the great deeds of God in many different native languages of the crowd. This perplexed them as they asked, "What does this mean?" (Acts 2:12). But others in the crowd were mocking and accusing the believers of being drunk. It was to this Jewish crowd in the city of Jerusalem, where Jesus had been killed just over seven weeks ago, that Peter delivered the sermon that launched the church. In terms of results—about 3,000 got saved that day—it was one of the greatest sermons ever preached.[8]

Acts 2:22-36 tells us that Peter stressed the importance of the Resurrection, because it fulfilled the prophecy of the Old Testament and was the final proof that Jesus was God's chosen one. Really, without the Resurrection there would have been no church. And these disciples were speaking not from hearsay or make-believe stories but from direct experiences of Jesus rising from torture, death on a cross, and the empty tomb.

After telling the listeners about the importance of Jesus and the significance of the Resurrection came the baptizing of believers. In his teachings, Peter is clear that the baptism of the Holy Spirit is for everyone, with these three simple steps: (1) repent; (2) be water baptized; and (3) receive the Holy Spirit. Peter was speaking to the people on that Day of Pentecost long ago, and he was speaking to us today.

We have in Jesus Christ, who gives us a glimpse of God, God present with us. In Jesus we have the prime example, a perfect model of what it means to fully live in the freedom and with the grace that only God can give. We have the Resurrection, which is the confirmation that Jesus is and was of God. We accept that we sin and continue to sin. We miss the mark and cannot act without putting ourselves and our bias in the picture. For this we need to repent and ask for forgiveness. This means that we turn away from whatever keeps us from being wholly God-focused and turn toward God. It is then we can be baptized with water in the name of the Father, the Son, and the Holy Spirit and join the community of faith, the body of Christ, actively working to transform the world.

> Then the eleven disciples went to Galilee, to the mountain where Jesus had told them to go. When they saw him, they worshiped him; but some doubted. Then Jesus came to them and said, "All authority in heaven and on earth has been given to me. Therefore go and make disciples of all nations, baptizing them in the name of the Father and of the Son and of the Holy Spirit, and teaching them to obey everything I have commanded you. And surely I am with you always, to the very end of the age. (Matthew 28:16-20, NIV)

Living as the Church

The believers prayed. They listened. Then they heard and received power from the Spirit and responded by teaching, preaching, and baptizing others so they, in turn, could tell others. And they were off . . . creating new believers and expanding this new community of faith—the church. But how? Acts 2:42-47 offers some answers, which become a blueprint for other fellowships of believers—churches— that is still relevant for today. To be faithful to the teachings of Jesus, churches should take these steps:

1. *Learn*—be active in continual study about God through the Scriptures.

2. *Align with God*—let your mission and vision line up with God's.

3. *Invite fellowship*—accept the value of all people; function as a healthy family of God, a band of brothers and sisters, regardless of such things as social status, race, or creed.

4. *Pray*—speak to and with God; intercede and advocate for the well-being of even those who are enemies.

5. *Be reverent*—respect God and God's world and fellow creatures.

6. *Expect great things*—espouse a community where good things happen, and attempt those things that you can do only with God's help.

7. *Share*—live with a sense of responsibility for one another and the world. A Christian could not bear to have too much when others have too little.

8. *Worship*—the Spirit of God is there when two or more are present.

9. *Be joyful*—a gloomy Christian is a contradiction in terms. Joy is a fruit of the Spirit and an indication of God's presence.

10. *Witness*—a community of faithful people shine with a light that all can see.

11. *Grow*—grow in faith and mission. Let your church blossom and flourish as it does its part to bring in God's kingdom.

Looking at these eleven descriptors, how does my church and your church fare? These were characteristics of the early church; shouldn't they also be characteristics of churches today? Where in our churches does the light of the Holy Spirit shine through? Where is the Holy Spirit still hovering, waiting to hatch new light? What is holding our churches back from being like the early church?

Living in the Power
of the Holy Spirit

The book of Acts gives us the mighty winds and shows us the power of the Holy Spirit. It jump-started Jesus's followers and propelled them to expand the audience for God's message of love, forgiveness, justice, healing, and freedom. But it isn't nor has it ever been an easy task to convince a doubting world.

From the book of John, we learn that Jesus knew the Christian life would be difficult and would be a struggle, so he sent help in the form of the Holy Spirit. Jesus said:

> "If you love me, you will keep my commandments. And I will ask the Father, and he will give you another Advocate, to be with you forever. This is the Spirit of truth, whom the world cannot receive, because it neither sees him nor knows him. You know him, because he abides with you, and he will be in you." (John 14:15-17, NRSV)

Interestingly, the Greek word for advocate is *parakletos*, which is largely untranslatable. Various Bible versions use the words "Helper" and "Comforter," but translated literally it means "someone who is called in." I find that even more powerful, our Advocate, our Helper, is someone called in by God to remain among us and within us. When looking at the word, "we get a much better understanding of what Jesus is communicating. Essentially, he is saying that *the Holy Spirit is permanently called closely alongside each of us to provide coaching, direction, instruction, and counsel in our life journey,*" wrote John Bevere.[9] Jesus is saying that he's sending us on a hard task; convincing the world of these truths will be difficult. But Jesus is calling in reinforcements. When the world does not recognize God, the Holy Spirit will make the way clearer. Our role is to keep true and be faithful to God.

Jesus is also saying that if someone doesn't believe in God, they can't receive the Holy Spirit. God does not force Godself on any of us. Jesus knocks at the door of our hearts, but we must open and let God in. The choice, the decision to follow or not follow, is up to us. But make no mistake: God is always near and ready to help. If you expect to hear from God, pray for God to speak to you. This takes setting time aside to connect to God. Then we wait, in expectation, being open to the wonderful things the Spirit can do with and through us. God is faithful to us and will keep promises whether or not we are faithful. The good news is that we only need come as we are, ready to receive.

Then, in John 15 Jesus pushes us into a deeper relationship, encouraging us to be witnesses for Christ:

> "When the Advocate [Helper] comes, whom I will send to you from the Father, the Spirit of truth who comes from the Father, he will testify on my behalf. You also are to testify because you have been with me from the beginning." (John 15:26-27, NRSV)

The Holy Spirit also lures us to respond in our daily living, our witness. Christian witness comes from someone who has direct experience, like the disciples, or from long, personal experience of being with Christ. Our ability to witness comes from an inner conviction, which comes from personal intimacy with Christ. Our witness is our outward testimony, helping others know about Christ. To be witnesses for Christ in the world, we need personal intimacy, inner conviction, and outward testimony of our faith. But we also need the community of faith for support and encouragement. And while we'll never understand everything, if we tell the truth of what we've experienced, with the Spirit's guidance, that is enough.

> "I have much more to say to you, more than you can now bear. But when he, the Spirit of truth, comes, he will guide you into all the truth. He will not speak on his own; he will speak only what he hears, and he will tell you what is yet to come." (John 16:12-13, NIV)

God is active and continually reveals new truths to and for us. Have you ever reread a scripture and thought, *I haven't thought of it that way before?* Have you heard a sermon that was just what you needed to hear at that time? Have you read something in a book that brought you a new understanding or appreciation? It's God whispering in your ear. It's God guiding you to new truths, with the promise that there is more yet to come.

If you're thinking, *I'm not there yet. I don't feel comfortable heading out and talking with others about God. I don't feel like I'm ready to hear the Holy Spirit,* take heart. It's a process, and we'll talk more in the upcoming chapters about next steps. "As the caterpillar finds its new ability to fly, we should be thrilled over our Spirit-empowered ability to live differently and faithfully. Isn't this what the Scriptures speak of? Isn't this what we've all been longing for?" encourages Francis Chan.[10]

This next story dramatically demonstrates how responding to the Holy Spirit can change lives. It shows living out the Scriptures faithfully by listening, hearing, and then responding to the Spirit.

Listen—Hear—Respond

It had been a busy day. Our family was preparing for a long, out-of-state trip, and I was also planning a presentation to deliver to thirty people. With one last stop on my list, I pulled into a gas station to fill my car with gas. The evening was beautiful, and even though it was already late and growing darker, I paused to breathe in the unusually cool summer air.

It was then that I noticed a woman pacing back and forth around the gas station parking lot, nervously opening and closing her phone. A peace came over me, and a voice clearly said, "*Ask her if she needs anything.*"

The woman was in her early twenties and had dark hair pulled up in a bun. Going up to the woman, I asked, "Are you okay? Do you need anything?" She told me she was looking for the bus station and that she needed to get to Minneapolis. "Well, you're close to the city bus, but you're a long way from the bus station. Do you need a ride?" It didn't take her long to agree, and she headed toward my car.

When she got into my car, she completely broke down. Through sobs and tears she told me that a man had befriended her, but it led to her being controlled and trapped in a hotel. He had been selling her for sex. My heart froze, and sadness fell over me. She showed me the website. There she was—an online advertisement for human trafficking and sexual exploitation.

All she had were the clothes on her back and the cell phone she'd taken from the man [when she escaped]. As we drove to the bus station, I told her that we needed to call the police. The woman was so afraid and kept echoing, "No." I just kept repeating, "You are safe. The police can help you." I think why she finally relented and let me make the call was because she knew another woman was still trapped in the hotel.

When we arrived at the bus station, the police weren't there yet. A white SUV roared into the bus station. We sat low in my car, and soon he took off. It was her tormentor. After about ten minutes the police arrived; she was able to tell her story, and eventually they got her on a bus to go home.

The next day, my mom called and said I was famous. Without saying my name, it was announced on the news that help from a local Good Samaritan led to two women being rescued from sex trafficking and a man heading to prison.

It was so clear to me that this was the Holy Spirit. Standing outside and enjoying the evening, I was not distracted by the world and was able to clearly hear that I needed to ask this woman if everything was okay. I felt safe and completely at peace about approaching the woman. I just responded to the nudge of God.

—ND

The Holy Spirit and Jesus

We turn now to the Holy Spirit and Jesus. The Holy Spirit impacted Jesus's life and ministry. We specifically see it in his baptism by John, the Transfiguration, and Jesus's and his disciples' experience in the garden of Gethsemane. As we look at these three transformative moments, I will list the scriptures and encourage you to read them all. Each scripture reference is slightly different and brings a clearer understanding to these influential events.

The Baptism of Jesus: Matthew 3:13-17; Mark 1:9-11; Luke 3:21-22; John 1:29-34

Jesus responded to the call to begin his ministry when he was about thirty—a mature man. Although we don't know for sure, we can assume that Jesus waited for God's call in Nazareth—his hometown— helping around the house, in the carpenter's shop, and probably in the family garden. Jesus may have been a carpenter, or maybe a stone-mason; the word for both is the same in Aramaic, the language that common people generally spoke. In any event, Jesus lived with his family in humble circumstances.

Jesus followed God's beckoning to the river Jordan, where he saw his cousin John baptizing repentant Jews. Jesus then asked John to baptize him. Surprised, John felt as though Jesus should baptize him. But as soon as Jesus was baptized and came out from the wa-ter, the "heavens were opened," according to Matthew 3:16, and the Spirit of God descended like a dove, and a voice came from heaven and said, "This is my Son, the Beloved, with whom I am well pleased" (v. 17, NRSV).

Matthew's record, in particular, of Jesus's baptism makes it clear— Jesus is the Chosen One sent from God. The Holy Spirit will equip Jesus for his journey and will do so with love, symbolized by the gen-tleness of a dove. This powerful testimony by the Holy Spirit marks Je-sus's entry into ministry, as he transitioned from standing in sawdust to standing with people as an itinerant preacher, teacher, and healer.

Jesus's Transfiguration: Matthew 17:1-8; Mark 9:2-8; Luke 9:28-36; 2 Peter 1:16-18

As a preacher, teacher, and healer, Jesus attracted a lot of attention to himself and his disciples. The disciples tried to take in what Jesus told them, but they were often confused by what it was all about. The disciples even asked the same kinds of questions that we often ask, "Who is this Jesus, and what does it mean to follow him?"

While crowds flocked to Jesus, the religious authorities were be-ginning a plot to kill him. Who knew being a follower of this man could be so dangerous? Perhaps to steady his disciples, Jesus took three of the leaders—Peter, James, and John—up a high mountain in an attempt to explain who he was. In a moment, Jesus changed right before them. His face "shone like the sun, and his clothes became dazzling white" (Matthew 17:2, NRSV). The three disciples reacted with fear, but a voice came from a cloud and said, "This is my Son, the Beloved; with him I am well pleased; listen to him!" (v. 5, NRSV).

This was an important mid-course check-in. Jesus told his disciples of his impending death. The disciples had seen Jesus perform miracles and maneuver through difficult situations, but news of his death was especially disconcerting. If he were to die, could he really be the Messiah? The Transfiguration was a dramatic demonstration of God's intent, and the message to the disciples was clear—Jesus is holy and is of God; stay the course, keep your faith, listen, and the Holy Spirit will be with you.

Garden of Gethsemane: Matthew 26:36-46; Mark 14:32-42; Luke 22:39-46

Jesus knew the time of his death was near, so after a last meal with his followers, he retreated to a familiar place with his closest disciples, the same three who were with him at the Transfiguration. He needed their prayerful support. Jesus was filled with anguish knowing that he was soon to be betrayed, arrested, tortured, and crucified. So, he prayed fervently to God to give him a reprieve. "Let this cup pass from me," he said (Matthew 26:39). But the disciples failed him. They lacked stamina; instead of praying, they kept falling asleep.

Luke tells us that an angel came to Jesus as he was praying. Angels are God's messengers. This angel was sent to comfort and strengthen Jesus through the Holy Spirit's gentle whispers and let him know that God was with him, that he was not alone in his suffering and he wouldn't be alone as he faced the future. Instead of running away from what was coming, Jesus submitted to and trusted in God's will. But not without struggle, as evidenced by his sweating drops of blood. Yet we also know the end of the story. We have that luxury, while the dozing disciples could not. We know that God held the ultimate trump card—resurrection. Jesus rose from the dead. Nothing can defeat God, not even death.

Jesus's baptism, transfiguration, and Gethsemane experience show us how God acts through the Holy Spirit. In these scenes from the life of Jesus, we can see the promise, power, and presence of God in action—the promise that began at the river Jordan and culminates in a life-giving fountain for all of us.

Conclusion

In this chapter we focused on discovering the wind and whispers of the Holy Spirit through the Word of God in Scripture. There were three main areas of focus for our understanding. We looked at Genesis to show that the Holy Spirit was a part of the story from the very beginning. We worked through Acts 2 to show the spectacular force of the Spirit. From John we read about the help the Spirit provided to inspire and birth the church, through Peter's sermon and people's response through baptism.

Let Us Pray

You may have heard of the Apostles' Creed. A creed is a set of fundamental beliefs. While not written by the disciples or early apostles, this creed is the church's oldest. The Apostles' Creed goes back to at least AD 140 and sums up our principal beliefs. There are some variations, but it is meant to serve as a statement that summarizes our faith.

Join me in this creed as a closing prayer for the chapter.

> I believe in God, the Father Almighty,
> maker of heaven and earth;
> And in Jesus Christ his only Son, our Lord;
> who was conceived by the Holy Spirit,
> born of the Virgin Mary,
> suffered under Pontius Pilate,
> was crucified, dead, and buried;
> the third day he rose from the dead;
> he ascended into heaven,
> and sitteth at the right hand of God the Father Almighty;
> from thence he shall come to judge the quick and the dead.
> I believe in the Holy Spirit,
> the holy catholic* church,
> the communion of saints,
> the forgiveness of sins,
> the resurrection of the body,
> and the life everlasting. Amen.

(*universal)

Reflection Questions

1. Why do you think it is important to include the Holy Spirit at the beginning of the Bible?

2. Put yourself in the places of the core believers who experienced the rushing wind, tongues of fire, and speaking in other tongues. What are your feelings? What are your questions?

3. In the summary of the characteristics of the early church, which

does your church do well? Which does your church need to work on? How can you help?

4. Why is baptism important? What is your responsibility in the baptism of others?

5. Has God revealed something to you in a scripture, sermon, or book? Why does God reveal things in progression, not all at one time?

CONNECTING TO THE MYSTERY OF THE HOLY SPIRIT

I want you woven into a tapestry of love, in touch with everything there is to know of God. Then you will have minds confident and at rest, focused on Christ, God's great mystery

—Colossians 2:2-3, *The Message*

Listen—Hear—Respond

How this story came to me would require a flowsheet, Venn diagram, and advanced algebraic formulas. Trust me when I say the Holy Spirit was completely a part of this connection. What I discovered were two families woven together in a tapestry of love, each of whom experienced the mystery of God.

The relationship of these two families started through Burdell and Brett. These two husbands were connected by their families' tradition of raising Angus cattle. Their wives, Tammy G. and Tammy M., knew each other casually but had no idea that their lives would become so entwined. The two women would come to share much more than a first name.

Tammy G. and Burdell were excited to have their first child. She was having some high blood pressure issues, so their baby boy was delivered by C-section. They couldn't decide on a name; and while at first they weren't totally sold on the name Nathaniel, which means "gift for God," they finally decided on it and brought their gift home.

Nathaniel seemed to be a normal, healthy baby; but at almost two months, he started having green diapers and wouldn't eat. Tammy G. took him to the doctor, who suggested changing formula. Soon after the doctor's appointment, however, Nathaniel was in his swing but wouldn't stop crying. Tammy G. held him to her chest. He reached and grabbed her cross necklace, as he often did, and he calmed down. She laid him down in the crib, but soon realized his back wasn't moving; he wasn't breathing! She screamed, and Burdell began CPR on his son. Tammy G. called 911. She was on her knees, praying, and they waited . . . and waited for the ambulance. It always seems like an eternity when you're waiting.

They got to the hospital, and the doctor came to them, knelt in front of them, and simply said, "He's gone." Their gift from God had an undetected heart issue, and he had basically outgrown his heart's ability to sustain him. There was nothing anyone could have done.

"I didn't want to go to the hospital, and when I went, I didn't want to hold him. I regret that now, but I was so sad and so mad at God," said Tammy G. "Burdell got soft and I got hard. I was mad at everyone. I prayed so hard to God, and God didn't save my baby. One day I even stood outside in a snowstorm and threw eggs against a fence. I was just so angry."

Weaving a Tapestry of Love

Soon after, the pastor came to be with them. "I remember thinking, *He better not quote scripture or I'll lose it*," reflected Tammy G. "But what he did do was cry. He cried with us. This simple act, being with us, started to mend my heart."

Tammy M. felt she needed to be at the funeral, and further, to be at the cemetery when Nathaniel was buried. In fact, she was the last to leave. Tammy M. gave Tammy G a hug and thought to herself that she could never survive losing a child. "I was at a point where I was praying to God for a good friend. We didn't know each other that well, but I felt drawn to Tammy G." The Holy Spirit began weaving a tapestry of love.

A while after the loss of Nathaniel, Tammy G. had received a card from a woman on how to be grateful. "At first, I was mad; how could I possibly be grateful?" Tammy G. said. "And then I realized that this woman was unable to have children. While I was still so sad, I realized—I got to carry my child; I got to hold my child; I got to become a mom, while this woman can never have a baby. It was a turning point for me. Life isn't going to be fair, but I can be grateful. Okay, God, I don't understand, but I'm going to trust you." This mystery allowed her to begin to reach out in love to other women who had lost their children. This ministry touched many lives and helped make the comfort of the Holy Spirit present for other grieving parents.

Years passed, and Burdell's family was holding a final Angus bull sale. Tammy G., who wasn't feeling well, headed to the car to drive home. But Burdell called out and asked her to come back—a woman wanted to see her. Tammy G. returned to find a young woman, who said, "Tammy, you saved my life twenty-three years ago. You sent me a card with a booklet after I lost my baby, and you also included your phone number. I called you. You'd just had your second baby, and I remember you named her Hope. You were willing to talk me through this, telling me what had happened in your life—your loss. Your card and willingness to listen saved my life. I needed you to know. I want to thank you."

～

It was Mother's Day, and the youth were doing a Mother's Day program at church. "I remember looking at my daughter, Samantha, and she had such a big smile on her face," said Tammy M. "They sang the song 'Trading My Sorrows.'" After church the family went on a picnic, then to a family member's house, and then it was time to go home.

"Our two daughters, Elizabeth and Samantha, were right ahead of us as we caravanned home," recalled Brett, the dad. Both cars were about a mile from home, when as their daughters were approaching an intersection, Brett and Tammy could see the semitruck. Brett yelled, "Oh my God!" And like a slow-motion picture, they watched the collision.

Elizabeth walked out of the car, but Samantha did not. From that point on things got blurry. What they do remember is Brett got in the car with Samantha, but they couldn't get her out—the door wouldn't open. "I could hear her heart beating, but she wasn't breathing. After a bit, she took one deep breath, and then I knew in my heart that she was gone," Brett said, tearfully recalling the day. Later, he said, "Tammy got to bring Samantha into this world, and I helped bring her home to Jesus."

A neighbor called 911. Tammy M. was lying in the ditch, pleading with God not to take her daughter. And they waited. It seems like an eternity when you are waiting.

The ambulance arrived, and their neighbor drove the family to the hospital. Others showed up to support them. There were tears and there were prayers.

The doctor came out, knelt in front of them, and said, "I'm so sorry." Tammy M. remembers she just wanted to be with her daughters. "Elizabeth was in one room, Samantha was in the other room, and we just kept trading rooms, back and forth, to be with our daughters," Tammy M. recalls. "All I could do was lay my head on Samantha's stomach and cry."

Then came the important, but difficult, decision about organ donation. "I sort of went into shock. I couldn't make a decision. I still was thinking, *I don't want to leave the hospital without both of my daughters.* I knew we had to make a decision, but I was frozen." They came to the decision that their daughter could help so many others. "Honestly, I really wasn't at peace with our decision until later. I was going through Samantha's book bag and found a bookmark on organ donation and knew this was something Samantha would have wanted." In the shock and deep sorrow, God was weaving another tapestry of love.

The next few days were a blur. Tammy G. knew she had to be with Tammy M. "She wouldn't leave me alone," says Tammy M., with a smile. "She'd follow me around our house with a half piece of toast and tell me I had to eat something." One mother's heart knowing what the other mother's heart needed—loving presence.

People came in droves. There were cars up and down the driveway, in the yard, on the gravel road. People wanted to be with the family. There were some side conversations about the accident and the truck driver, a young man from the Hutterite colony. A Hutterite colony is a Germanic religious community. Its members live together and support themselves largely through agriculture and selling produce. The Hutterites are familiar to people in the upper Midwest and are easily spotted. The men traditionally wear black pants, suspenders, and dress shirts. The women wear long dresses and always have head coverings, traditionally in polka dots.

Tammy G. remembers how loud it was in the house, but it suddenly grew gentle. A young man in suspenders, followed by his sisters in dresses and head coverings, was coming up the steps. The young man was visibly shaking. Brett and Tammy M. did something holy and unexplainable and without any hesitation—they met the young man on the steps and embraced him.

"I couldn't believe what I was seeing," reflects Tammy G. "I was in complete awe, and you could feel the presence of the Holy Spirit. We were all able to witness this powerful act of forgiveness and compassion."

Through hugs and tears, the young man made a request: Could he and his sisters sing for Samantha and her friends and family? They went into the living room and sang. They sang that day. They sang at the visitation. They came regularly over many weeks to sing for the family. And every Mother's Day since, the family goes to Samantha's grave. Every Mother's Day since, they have found a rose and a note written in German on the grave. The Holy Spirit continues to offer a healing balm.

God continued to weave love into and through the families.

Sometimes God puts our mind at rest by helping us see and make connections. "In 1 Kings 19, the scripture verse talks about how God was not in the powerful wind, not in an earthquake, not in the fire, but how God came in the gentle whisper," Brett related. "We learned to see the Holy Spirit in small ways, things you might ordinarily overlook. But God was in those signs."

At the cemetery, there was also a gathering of classmates to launch pastel-colored balloons for Samantha. The cemetery is about ten miles south of the farm, where the family lives. There was a strong north wind that day, so they watched the balloons fly and quickly disappear to the south. Tammy M. had been praying for a sign from God. The day after the funeral, there was a light blue balloon hovering over the cattle yard. Without hesitation, their son went out to grab the balloon, and the family believes that God put the balloon there for them. As Tammy M. said, "I think all the balloons reached heaven and Samantha sent one back for us." Given the usual wind pattern, how the balloon could possibly have gotten to their farm is a mystery, but it gave them something to hold on to.

Samantha loved butterflies, so they had her headstone sculpted into the shape of a butterfly. Later, when they had the first family picture taken after Samantha's death, a butterfly flew into the group and landed on Tammy M. "Guess Samantha still wanted to be part of the family photo. She sent us another sign that she was still with us," said Tammy.

After the accident, Burdell announced to his music classes that he was canceling practices this week due to the death of the daughter of close friends. After class, a student stopped and asked if she could speak to him. She asked Burdell if he knew if this daughter had donated her organs? When Burdell said yes, she added, "I think I received one of her corneas."

It was Mother's Day and the one-year anniversary of Samantha's death. The family was trying to decide where to have lunch and finally chose a local Perkins restaurant. Another family was also trying to decide where to have lunch and finally chose the same Perkins restaurant. It was busy that day, being Mother's Day. While waiting to be seated, a young woman came to Brett and Tammy M. and asked if they were the Millers. Tammy M. said, "We knew at once we were looking at Samantha's eyes." The Holy Spirit guided and wove them together, so they could see Samantha living on through another person.

Years later, Elizabeth was expecting her first child. She and her husband decided not to find out the gender of their baby. A first grandchild and healthy baby girl was born. You can probably guess what they named her—Samantha. Apparently, she not only looks like her aunt Samantha, as Elizabeth and Tammy M. often remark, but she carries herself the same way and has her personality. The Holy Spirit wove them together, giving comfort and encouragement along the way.

God's ways are mysterious. But the Spirit of God reaches out to us, helping us, through grace, to be faithful. It doesn't mean that every path is straight; it just means God will journey with us and can put our minds at rest.

Both families would want you to know that this wasn't easy.

Both families would want you to know there are resources and help available. One family went through Christian counseling to help them navigate this new reality.

Both families would want you to know there were days that they didn't want to get out of bed. There were days that were dark.

Both families would want you to know that while it is hard, they still want to talk about their children.

Both families would want you to know that *you* have the ability to weave a tapestry of love, as their family and friends did for them—through prayers, through meals, through taking the time to walk with others.

Both families would want you to know they don't always understand the ways of God, but there comes a time when their minds were finally put at peace. It came when they focused on God and the works of the Holy Spirit.

> I want you woven into a tapestry of love, in touch with everything there is to know of God. Then you will have minds confident and at rest, focused on Christ, God's great mystery. (Colossians 2:2-3, *The Message*)

When we speak about the Holy Spirit, we may shrink back with questions and doubts that may arise. The Holy Spirit is that part of the Trinity that is most foreign to us. We are just not familiar, or we consider it a bizarre belief for the extremists or religious fanatics. The Holy Spirit may disturb us, because we are not used to thinking of God in this way. Just remember that the Holy Spirit is God, present with us. The Holy Spirit is God leading, comforting, and inspiring us so that we may be the people God intends us to be. This book is an attempt to connect with, know, understand, appreciate, and recognize the presence and power of the Holy Spirit—to seek and then bring the Holy Spirit along as our companion on life's path.

Before we talk about how, the more basic question might be why? Why connect to the Holy Spirit? Charles Stanley in *Living in the Power of the Holy Spirit* gives us two main reasons to connect: first to be a witness and second to do the ministry of Jesus Christ.

Living as God's Witness

The Holy Spirit enables us to be God's witnesses. No matter what profession or vocation we choose, the Spirit calls people to be witnesses for God. "Every believer can speak the name of Jesus in the marketplace, the hospital, the courtroom, the classroom, the family kitchen, the construction site, the factory floor, the sports arena, or any other place the believer may be," wrote Stanley.[11] All Christians are called to be witnesses, and the Holy Spirit provides us the tools. "The Holy Spirit gives us the wisdom, strength, comfort, and power to speak and act in a way that reflects Christ Jesus," Stanley continued.[12]

Doing the Ministry of God

Then the Holy Spirit enables us to do the ministry of God by imparting to us one or many spiritual or ministry gifts. Those gifts make us more attentive, so God can enable us to do amazing things in the name of God. Spiritual fruit are the effects of the gifts we are given and are listed in Galatians 5. They include love, joy, peace, patience, kindness, goodness, gentleness, faithfulness, and self-control. We will dig deeper into gifts and fruit in later chapters.

As disciples and followers of Jesus Christ, we are not called to be the judge or jury, not the prosecuting or defense attorney, but a *witness*. We are called to share our experience of God—what we've seen, what we've experienced, what we know, and what we have done as a result of our relationship with God. The Holy Spirit uses our witness to impact others. A witness always speaks in the first person, "I" or "me." If we use the second person, "you," we are no longer a witness but seeking to be judge or jury, telling others what to believe or what to do or how to respond. "The Holy Spirit in us gives us the strength, power, and wisdom to be active in our God-ordained service to others," says Stanley.[13] We are called to be witnesses by doing God's work in the world to help bring in God's kingdom; and with this goal in mind, the Holy Spirit provides the tools and the power. That is why we want to connect, because we can't do it on our own.

Now, you might be asking, "But how? How do I connect with the Holy Spirit?" Billy Graham, in the book *The Holy Spirit: Activating God's Power in Your Life*, shares this story:

> An Eskimo fisherman came to town every Saturday afternoon. He always brought his two dogs with him. One was white and the other was black. He had taught them to fight on command. Every Saturday afternoon in the town square the people would gather, and these two dogs would fight, and the fisherman would take bets. On one Saturday the black dog would win; another Saturday, the white dog would win—but the fisherman always won! His friends began to ask him how he did it. He said, "I starve one and feed the other. The one I feed always wins because he is stronger."[14]

I ask you a question: Are you being fed or are you starving? Are you being fed by prayer, reading Scripture, listening to sermons, reading thought-provoking books, sharing and connecting with others, serving to make the world a better place, giving to causes important to you, and being open to the power of the Holy Spirit? If so, you are being fed; and when you're fed, you're stronger and winning. If you're starving, you're losing.

Connecting with the Spirit of God starts with being fed. Fill yourself first. Let's look at four specific steps to connect with the Holy Spirit: become aware, prepare, ask, recognize.

Become Aware

As introduced in the first chapter, the first thing we need to do in becoming aware is to see the Holy Spirit as a person—as someone, not something. When we are aware that the Holy Spirit is someone, not just a nebulous concept, we can build and foster a relationship. Go back and review the end of chapter 1, as to who the Holy Spirit is—a person of the Trinity, eternal and holy—who prays for us, intercedes on our behalf, is all-powerful, always present, and all-knowing.

Don't worry about understanding everything; just be aware that the Holy Spirit is meant to be part of our lives and is God. Our obligation is to be aware. "The Holy Spirit indwells you to nudge you, prod you, push you, mold you, remake you, and fashion you in the fullness of all that God has for you," wrote Charles Stanley. "The Holy Spirit is at work in you to be the developer of your life—bringing all of your talents and abilities to the fullness of their use both naturally and spiritually."[15]

I love the word *indwell*, which means "permanently present in someone's soul or mind." Maybe this is a strange illustration, but a few years ago I developed shingles. I had a rash and pain on one side of my back that lasted a couple of weeks. When the doctor diagnosed my shingles, he said it comes from the chicken pox virus. Once you've had chicken pox, the virus remains in the body's nerve cells and, for reasons not well understood, it may reactivate later in life.

The Spirit of the Lord indwells within our cells, permanently present in our bodies, ready to be called upon at any moment. To connect with the Holy Spirit, we start with awareness, and unlike shingles, our hope is to let the power of the Holy Spirit be made evident in our lives. "Guard, through the Holy Spirit who dwells in us, the treasure which has been entrusted to you" (2 Timothy 1:14, NASB1995).

Prepare

"Before you are filled with the Holy Spirit you must be sure that you can be filled.... This Spirit-filled life is not a special, deluxe edition of Christianity, wrote A. W. Tozer. "It is part and parcel to the total plan of God for [God's] people."[16] Preparing to connect with the Holy Spirit is not something that is limited to special persons. It is available to everyone. We have to desire to be filled, and then we must prepare ourselves to be filled.

> Therefore, I urge you, brothers and sisters, in view of God's mercy, to offer your bodies as a living sacrifice, holy and pleasing to God—this is your true and proper worship. Do not conform to the pattern of this world but be transformed by the renewing of your mind. Then you will be able to test and approve what God's will is— his good, pleasing and perfect will. (Romans 12:1-2, NIV)

A. W. Tozer, in his book *How to Be Filled with the Holy Spirit*, wrote at length about preparing ourselves for the Holy Spirit to bless, lift, purify, and direct our lives. But there are three signs that we may not be ready. First, we may want Christianity as an "insurance policy" against anything bad happening to us. It is not. We think that if we live "reasonably well" and call ourselves Christians, we are paying the premium for a guarantee that God will bless us. Not ready yet.

Second, we might feel that religion is a social and not a spiritual concern. We go to church, but we go to be seen—so we can feel that we've done our duty or so we can just check it off our list. But that's as far as we go. The gospel of Christ is essential, and Christian truth working in human souls by the Holy Spirit makes Christians spiritual. Just a social outing? Not ready yet.

Third, we are more influenced by the world than by the Word of God. It is so hard not to be influenced by the world when we are bombarded with messages on television and social media—messages of *more*. The world has pleasures and tastes and influences that pull us away from God's will for our lives. If Scripture doesn't disturb and convict you, maybe you're not ready yet.

But if you are ready, prepare the way. It doesn't mean a perfect life. It doesn't mean a sinless life. It means we're aware and now ready to prepare the path for the Holy Spirit. Charles Stanley says,

> When the Holy Spirit indwells our lives, [the Spirit] changes our desires, our needs, our innermost goals—not necessarily eliminating our desires, needs, or goals, but *changing them*. Even so, the saying is true, "old habits die hard." Most of us have developed a habit of thinking in certain ways, acting in certain ways, and responding to certain situations in certain ways. It takes time and intentional effort to change those patterns of thinking and behaving.[17]

We are aware of the Holy Spirit. We prepare ourselves to be open to the Holy Spirit. Now ask.

Ask

"So I say to you: Ask and it will be given to you; seek and you will find; knock and the door will be opened to you. For everyone who asks receives; the one who seeks finds; and to the one who knocks, the door will be opened." (Luke 11:9-10, NIV)

Ask the Spirit to be part of your life. Charles Stanley provides us a focus and prayer:

> We do this by actively and verbally placing our trust in the Lord, saying, "I need You, Holy Spirit, to help me become and do all that God has created me to be and do. I need You, Holy Spirit, to work in me in such a way that I will want to accomplish and be able to accomplish all that You have purposed for me to do in my life."[18]

To begin, ask these four questions:

1. What do you want me to do? Be open to hearing the Holy Spirit.

2. How do you want me to act? Ask the Holy Spirit to show you how to accomplish the tasks before you.

3. When do you want me to act? When you act can be as important as how you act and what you do. Listen for God's timing.

4. How can I best represent you today? Prayerfully ask the Holy Spirit to mold you into a likeness of Christ.

Recognize

I would like to learn just one thing from you: Did you receive the Spirit by the works of the law, or by believing what you heard? (Galatians 3:2, NIV)

We are aware of the Holy Spirit. We prepare ourselves and are open to the Holy Spirit. We pray and ask for the Holy Spirit to be part of our lives. Now we recognize and see the Holy Spirit woven in and through our lives.

A. W. Tozer reminds us to cultivate the art of recognizing the presence of the Spirit everywhere.[19] Get acquainted with the Holy Spirit, and then begin to look for the Spirit's presence. When you wake up in the morning, instead of scrolling through your phone or checking your social media—while you eat your eggs and drink your coffee—think of God.

Conclusion:
I Saw God Today

My wife and I started a ministry on the island of La Gonâve, which is just off the coast of Haiti. This connection morphed into a nonprofit called LaGonave Alive, and our focus is in the areas of education and health care, particularly for supporting women, children, and the elderly. Consequently, we have a school, a clinic, feeding programs, and a Christmas celebration. We distribute food, clothing, and school supplies, and we try to make a small difference in that corner of our world.

For the last several years, I have led teams to meet the wonderful people and maybe help a little bit. On one of our trips, I asked team members to recognize God throughout the day and be ready to discuss "where I saw God today." Our evening discussions were rich. Following this particular trip, I put together a picture and reflection booklet and included a few of those stories below. My purpose is to energize you to recognize God and the Holy Spirit, first in small things, then in all things.

⁓

I saw God today in the old woman who sweeps the street each day. This stretch of road is filled with people, donkeys, and motorcycles, which serve as taxis. Even though on the next day there would again be leaves, papers, and other messes, she continues to sweep with her old homemade broom. Each day we bring new problems to God. Each day God tends to our needs and cleans up when we have failed. A God who cares for us, even though we will continue to mess up our part of the street. I saw God in an old woman today.

⁓

I saw God today in a boy with many problems, whose long, dirty shirt didn't cover up his body or his odor. His life is filled with taunts and being pushed aside. All he wanted to do was touch my white legs. No matter if it is in the market or on the path, he faces scolds and shoves. Jesus said when you do it to the least of these, you do it unto me. Who could be "least-er" than he?

⁓

I saw God today in the three-legged dog. In our compound was a three-legged dog who struggled to get under our gate but was able to move remarkably quickly. The dog let me know that we all have issues to overcome and we all need to do the best we can with what we have. Some of our problems are more difficult than others, but we all have struggles. I was thinking, what could be worse than being a three-legged dog in Haiti? Then I saw the one-armed man.

I saw God today in a donkey. I'm not sure there is an animal that works as hard as a donkey. In a place with little water or food, the donkey gets loaded down with huge bags of charcoal, piles of bananas, wood, or sometimes the owner. The person guiding the donkey frequently has to use a whip to coax the beast to continue in the right direction. When we went to the market, there was a "donkey parking lot" waiting for more work later in the day. A missionary said to me once, "The work that you do needs to always be about God and not about you as a person." Donkeys are great role models; they keep their head down and plod along day after day. The donkey, who occasionally needs some direction, does the heavy lifting without needing recognition. I saw God in the donkey today.

I saw God today in ants. I was feeling a bit overwhelmed one day with all the needs in Haiti. There is a never-ending stream of people who need and deserve help. My Haitian buddy wisely said, "Friend, your arm only stretches as long as it can." Then the ants came out of nowhere and took apart a dead moth within minutes. It reminded me that there are so many people who are interested and willing to help. When we work together, we aren't small; we can be a force. Our arms stretch farther.

Let Us Pray

Loving God and Holy Spirit
> I thank you today that you are deeply embedded in my
> cells.

That I simply need to be aware of you, to prepare for you,
> To ask you to be a part of my daily life, then recognize
> you in all things.

That is my hope, that is my prayer.
> To make you fully a part of all I am and do.

So I can be your witness and do what you ask.
> All for you and for your glory. Amen.

Reflection Questions

1. What struck you most about the opening story? How do you feel the Spirit played a role?

2. How can you best be a witness? How can you best do the ministry of Christ Jesus?

3. Are you ready to receive the Holy Spirit? If not, what would it take?

4. Become aware; prepare; ask; recognize. How do you understand these steps for your life?

5. Where did you see God today?

JOHN WESLEY AND THE HOLY SPIRIT

*The sum of all this is: The testimony of the Spirit
is an inward impression on the souls of believers,
whereby the Spirit of God directly testifies to
their spirit, that they are children of God.*

**—"The Witness of the Spirit, Discourse Two,"
a sermon by John Wesley**

John Wesley was short in physical stature but stood tall as a preacher, writer, theologian, and in his belief in the power of the Holy Spirit working in one's life. Wesley became a tireless evangelist; his prolific preaching and thousands of miles on foot and on horseback are well documented.

"John Wesley believed strongly in the power and working of the Holy Spirit in one's life. He held that each person is endowed by the Creator with the capacity to receive the Holy Spirit in his or her heart," wrote Arvest Lawson. Wesley believed he had no "extraordinary gifts."[20] Rather, he believed that he was just like everyone else, an ordinary person who could experience the power of the Holy Spirit in their lives. Chris Ritter says that Wesley "continually made the case that the 'normal' life of faith is infused with the power of the Holy Spirit."[21] The gifts and force of the Spirit are extraordinary, but they are available to ordinary people and expected to be part of our normal journey of faith.

Further, I resonate with John Wesley in his faith journey. He didn't have a dramatic conversion experience; he just realized that his "heart" was "strangely warmed" in what is known as his Aldersgate experience.[22] Wesley was a latecomer to his understanding of the Holy Spirit. Wesley struggled with doubts about his faith. His work in ministry wasn't always successful. All of these ring true in my life.

John Wesley (1703–1791), the founder of Methodism, wrote a book, later edited by Clare Weakley, entitled *The Holy Spirit and Power*. In it, Wesley tells us that he was an ordained minister in a family of ministers; he received a master's degree from Oxford and preached to faculty and students, but he felt he didn't have the faith he wanted or needed. He said: "This faith by the power of the Holy Spirit would come to me later. Then I would be able to lead many into the same powerful spiritual experience."[23]

Then in 1735, to gain the faith he coveted, Wesley signed on to be a missionary and headed to the American colonies. On a ship with him was a group of Germans—Moravian Christians. "There were twenty-six of these unusual Christians on the ship," wrote Wesley.[24] On their long and dangerous trip, they encountered three violent storms. Everyone was terrified for their lives, except those Germans.

The third storm, a hurricane, came with violence, rolling and rocking the boat from side to side, threatening to capsize the boat. Waves of water swept over the deck and poured in the portholes and down the hatches. Most passengers screamed and scrambled for safety, but the Germans, who had started their worship, calmly sang on. Wesley was amazed. He wondered how even the women and children could remain so calm in the storm. So, after the storm subsided, Wesley asked if their women and children were afraid. The leader said, "No. Our women and children are not afraid to die." After that experience, Wesley watched the Germans closely. "They were always busy, usefully employed, cheerful, and in good humor. They had done away with all strife, anger, bitterness, clamor, and evil-speaking. They walked and lived as true witnesses of Christ."[25] Even when one man was particularly critical of Wesley and his preaching, John continued to be intrigued by these Germans.

Wesley finally landed at the port in Savannah, Georgia, but "after two years of poor results in this chosen work, I thought it was time to leave the mission field. I took a ship home."[26] On the return trip, he had much time and solitude to think about Christianity, his faith, his unbelief. He felt that he had gone to the mission field to convert others but wondered if he, himself, didn't need to be converted to God.

The missionary work humbled and focused Wesley. Upon his return home, God also put Moravian Christians on his path "who had the faith which I sought."[27] Wesley had meetings and conversations with one of their influential leaders, Peter Bohler. As a result, along with studying Scripture, Wesley came to a new understanding of what it meant to experience God. "That faith transferred them from darkness into light, out of sin and fear into holiness and happiness." Wesley ends with this summation. "Here my disputing ended. I could now only cry out, 'Lord, help my unbelief.'"[28]

Wesley continues: "I had continued to seek this faith, though with some strange indifference, dullness, and coldness until May 24 [1738]." He then went very unwillingly to a Bible study held in a meeting house on Aldersgate Street in London. (The actual place is gone; there is still a plaque designating the site.) While listening to Martin Luther's preface to Paul's New Testament letter to the Romans,

Wesley wrote, "I felt my heart strangely warmed."[29] Wesley finally found the assurance of salvation that he craved.

Although Wesley sometimes downplayed his poignant experience, it is undeniable that from that point Wesley began speaking with a new energy and a heart for God. Preaching as many as three times a day, he declared the good news he felt deep within, and Methodism, as a movement, began in earnest. Wesley also became more deeply aware of the power of the Holy Spirit. He said, "The Holy Spirit began to move among us with amazing power when we met in His name."[30]

Wesley saw dramatic changes in people, often his fiercest critics, who "cried out in complete joy" or, in some cases, were "knocked to the ground." People were physically and spiritually healed because of the Holy Spirit. He met people in pain, with physical ailments, in prison, and on the streets. Through prayer and inviting the Spirit to bring peace and joy, Wesley said that "these unusual works of the Holy Spirit continue to follow and bless my ministry."[31] These experiences prompted Wesley to preach and write extensively about the Holy Spirit.

One of the gifts Wesley left for us was his admonition to expect the Holy Spirit in our ordinary and daily lives. He stressed that we can come to new understandings, even if we are believers. It's okay to doubt. That struggle may move us to deeper belief. Our responsibility is to remain faithful.

Listen—Hear—Respond

From Renee: I think the Holy Spirit is present and communicating with us all the time. The question is: Are we listening? The more you are plugged into God through prayer, Scripture, meditation, and—for me—time outdoors, the more I am able to think, act, hear, and reflect God's nature.

Similar to a marriage, where the two become one, the more I put into the relationship, the more we become alike. We don't merge into one person; rather, we become more of who we were meant to be when we are together. We operate out of a mutual respect and growing love. We do not argue over a lot of decisions, because after thirty-four years of marriage, we think similarly; we even dress alike too often. We settled many differences long ago, so now we can just move down life's road together. It's the same way in your relationship with God. I have found that when I don't put in the effort, I start to become selfish, and my listening ear starts to dull. I do not respond with a heart filled with the Holy Spirit.

There are many situations where the Holy Spirit has worked in and through me. One that stands out is on a build in Mexico with Casas por Cristo. It was windy; sand was blowing in my face, and every crevice of my body was filled with dirt and sweat. Our team was just finishing the house, and there was an ongoing competition between building teams. It was getting late; we were behind schedule, hungry, and thirsty; everyone was exhausted.

For several moments I felt this peace and contentment wash over me, this sense of being where God wanted me to be—despite the heat, wind, tiredness, and the fighting going on inside the house. I felt God smiling. Instead of a burning bush, it was the burning heat. Instead of a gentle breeze, the wind was blowing relentlessly, but God's presence was washing over me. This overwhelming peace was an affirmation that I was where I was called to be.

Sometimes the Holy Spirit speaks to me through a scripture

and an accompanying conviction from the Word. Sometimes it's a thought that flies through my head, and I know I must speak or do. I have felt God's presence and peace so thick in the valleys as I walked with a dying friend or family member. Other times it's just an affirmation of the Holy Spirit saying, "I got you, daughter."

How is the Holy Spirit present and communicating with us? Through grace and through the genuine gifts of the Spirit: joy, love, and humility.

The Gift of Joy

"John Wesley stressed again and again that one of the genuine gifts of the Holy Spirit is joy: joy deep down in the center of one's being; joy in the heart," wrote Arvest N. Lawson. "And according to Wesley, it is only the Holy Spirit who can bring this joy to one's heart and life."[32] When we lose joy, we lose the power of our belief.

I have always been amazed that we have grumpy Christians. Not the occasional grumpy but the perennial grumpy Christian. Move the worship service fifteen minutes? The sky is falling. Sit in my pew or seat? God only comes to me in one location. Persons who look different or dress different? Judged and cast aside. Where is the joy?

One of my favorite things about leading a team to Haiti is our reflection time each night. We talk about what happened during the day—where we saw God—and then we pose a question to the group. Each night a different person chooses the question. I have a book of questions that they can use, or the person can come up with their own question. It's a neat way to get to know everyone better and for the team to find out interesting things about one another.

The last night of a recent trip, one of the team members asked us to highlight the most memorable thing about our trip. We had a good week on La Gonâve—painting schoolrooms and benches, giving out food and other items, playing with kids, having a movie and popcorn night, hanging out with our Haitian friends—a lot of good memories. My memorable event was a night when I noticed the brilliant stars in the sky. The stars are so bright in Haiti, because they don't have many streetlights or ambient light from homes. It gave me a sense of awe of God's creation but also how much I appreciate being able to travel to La Gonâve. It isn't an easy or convenient place to get to, but I love the people there and appreciate that I can be a small part of their lives.

The person who suggested the question is also a pastor. His response has stuck with me. However, his reflection needs a bit of context. One afternoon we traveled up the mountain to a small village. Local doctors were holding a mobile clinic, and we went up to observe and to bring medical supplies and food. We loaded up supplies and seven of us in the back of a pickup. Now, the worst roads you've been on are some of the best on La Gonâve. It is a rocky, volcanic island, and the roads are almost indescribable. It took more than two hours to go about fifteen miles to this village.

About an hour into our journey, it began raining. I mean pouring. We were soaked to the core. After we arrived at the clinic, we gave out food and medical supplies and observed some of the difficult medical cases. The rain had let up, so I decided to load the team back up and head down the mountain. Not ten minutes into our trip, it began to rain. I mean pour—a deluge of rain. It was actually the first time I've ever been cold in Haiti. A young woman on our team, her hands turned purple. Being soaked for three hours, even in Haiti, makes you chilly.

I was sitting on the back corner of the pickup, along with my pastor friend. He and I could see the water cascading down the road behind us. It looked like a waterfall, water pouring over the rocks and chasing us down the hill. He and I would look at each other—and laugh. We'd look at other team members, drowned rats in the back of a pickup, and just laugh. A time when people could have been angry or disappointed or frustrated, and all we could do was laugh.

My pastor friend recalled this as his memorable event. He said he will use this memory when the sky is falling on him, when things are dark and bleak, when he is soaked from the problems of others, when people are sharing that they are angry or disappointed or frustrated—he can choose to laugh. Through it all, things will be better. The rain will stop. We will put on dry clothes. Our shoes will dry out. The sun will shine. We can laugh. There can be joy.

The Gift of Love

As our joy increases, so does our love. Wesley believed in a vertical dimension to love. He believed that out of one's love for God comes one's love for others. In other words, the horizontal dimension, loving others, was always secondary to loving God.[33]

Wesley taught that love should be "universal" and "disinterested."[34] Isn't that an awesome perspective? We need to love universally and not let differences or race or nationality interfere. We need to extend our love to all people, everywhere. This ability to love God and every human being is a gift of the Holy Spirit.

If you want to read a challenging book in the Bible, one that promotes universal and impartial love, pick the book of James. It's believed to be a letter written by James, a brother of Jesus, who at first didn't believe Jesus was the Messiah (John 7:5). Jesus pulled the "Messiah card" and proved his little brother wrong by appearing to him after the Resurrection (1 Corinthians 15:3-7). James later became an important figure in the early church and an ardent supporter of action and love with faith. But James was also critical of the way we live out our faith. He said, "With the tongue we praise our Lord and Father, and with it we curse human beings, who have been made in God's likeness" (James 3:9, NIV).

As I was working on a sermon for James 3, this verse stuck with me. James is peering into our lives and pointing out the hypocrisy of praising and cursing out of the same mouth. We praise God, and we should, but we curse those made in God's likeness. We use our mouths for the highest calling, blessing God, and the lowest evil, cursing those made in God's image.

I worry about what I see on social media. We've become so distant from loving everyone and seeing them as people made in God's likeness. We say that "they" are dangerous or "they" are scary, or "their" views are wrong. Who are "they"? Aren't all of us made in the image of God? How can we worship in comfortable places or pray in our comfortable homes, then reject those we see through the windows? We don't see the people harmed by Facebook posts. We don't see people in a spiteful tweet. We don't see people in the Instagram post meant to shame.

Years ago, we spent an afternoon on a beautiful, white-sand beach along the deep blue ocean in Barbados. A man came up to us selling necklaces and said, "Welcome to my office." I told the man his office had a better view than mine. I learned his name was Sunny and found out we were the same age. He loves creating jewelry and believes God rewards him when he stays busy and that Satan creeps in when he is idle. His mother has dementia, so Sunny's son has to stay with her during "office hours." This is his only source of income.

I'm not really sure why, but I asked Sunny how he is treated by the people who come to the beach. He responded, "People are usually nice, but I just want people to greet me even if they don't want to buy anything. Many people won't even acknowledge that I exist." Won't even "acknowledge that I exist"? Sunny, child of God, doesn't exist? Then who else doesn't exist? Immigrants? Elderly neighbors? People with difficult views? The person on the other side of a malicious post?

Dear God, control not only our words, but control our hearts; allow us to love.

══ The Gift of Humility ══

Wesley believed that there is no place for the sin of pride in our relationship with God. Lawson reminds us that "spiritual arrogance was totally foreign to the thinking of John Wesley. Such arrogance simply eclipses the working of the Holy Spirit in one's heart."[35]

Humility is not easy, but Wesley taught that it requires the attitudes of being obedient and submissive—obedient to remaining humble, submissive to being teachable. We then understand that God is in all, and we credit God for all. Ramona's story is an example of being obedient and submissive to the Spirit.

> It was a Sunday afternoon, and I was sitting out in the sun, reading, and praying for our kids. One was in college; one in high school; one in middle school. I was praying for their protection, that they would make good choices, and for them to honor God with their lives. I was praying but also, I was worrying.
>
> Very clearly, I heard, "Ramona, I know you love your children, but I love them more than you possibly ever could.

You can trust Me." I can't describe the absolute peace that filled my heart and mind! I knew it was the Holy Spirit. This clear message from the Spirit has forever changed the way I pray for my kids. I don't pray for particular jobs, homes, or things. Instead I pray that they will look to God and that God will provide and know what is best for them. I pray that they will love God with ALL their hearts, minds, and souls. What great peace and freedom there is in trusting that the Spirit will work through my children. There's also a great excitement in that because I know God's ideas are far better than anything I could ever come up with.

Joy, love, and humility—these are only three gifts of the Holy Spirit. Our responsibility is to accept them as gifts from God and use these gifts through the power of the Holy Spirit.

A friend of mine went through a cancer surgery and needed a ride across the state to his home. I said I'd be glad to drive him. It was a long day, five-plus hours there and five-plus hours home, but it was nice to be able to help a little. On the drive, I said to him, "Thank you for allowing me to help." He looked confused, and I explained that when people won't accept help, it denies *us* the ability to give.

Why are we so unwilling to accept a gift? Is it pride? False modesty? Stubbornness? A cultural ethic? A feeling that we won't be able to repay the giver or give something in return? In so many situations, we don't know how to help. Small gestures of kindness not only help the receiver, but they also help us, the givers. When we refuse to receive a gift, we deny people the opportunity to give. Give and accept the gifts of the Spirit of God.

It's Simply Grace

Beyond these gifts, to truly understand the Holy Spirit, we must understand Wesley's teachings about grace. In my book *Simply Grace: Everyday Glimpses of God*, I tried to simplify Wesley's concepts of grace and allow us to see grace playing out in our everyday lives.[36] Wesley introduced us to prevenient, justifying, and sanctifying grace, which is one of John Wesley's finest contributions to helping us understand how God interacts with us. Generally speaking, prevenient grace is the grace that "goes before"—that grace which precedes our action and reflects God's love for creation. Prevenient grace is love that is available regardless of what we've done or how we've lived. It is grace that goes before all else; it is love that is present for us, always available, and pulls us back to God.

As I have said, central to understanding prevenient grace is to understand John Wesley's view of God. Pure and simple, Wesley believed God is love. Wesley's focus is not on our sin or the fact that we need God because of our sin. The focus begins with love. It comes before all else and embraces us and pulls us to God regardless of our sin, mistakes, and missteps. It is also Wesley's belief that grace is active in us and around us. Even before we know God, God loves us. This is not, however, a view that is universally accepted. Some see sin as God's primary emphasis, and this theology focuses on what we do to seek God's forgiveness. Wesley believed the character of God is love. He spoke of the Holy Spirit as the agent of prevenient grace—the agent or force that makes God's grace available to us.

Our response to God's grace testifies to a change in our lives that comes as we accept Jesus Christ as our Savior. This conversion experience is what Wesley called "justifying grace." Some refer to it as rebirth, new life, being born again, or regeneration. We accept God's forgiveness, we testify to a change, and we begin to live differently.

Then we take steps to deepen our relationship with God, what Wesley called "sanctifying grace." John Wesley preached often about the sanctifying work of the Holy Spirit. The goal of this sanctification is to make a us a living portrait of Jesus. It isn't a perfect or even a straight path but steps, even small steps, to living more like Jesus.

Mark Olson highlights that Wesley "emphasized the person and work of the Holy Spirit at each stage in the process of salvation." He quotes Wesley:

> I believe the infinite and eternal Spirit of God, equal with the Father and the Son, to be not only perfectly holy in himself, but the immediate cause of all holiness in us: enlightening our understandings, rectifying our wills and affections, renewing our natures, uniting our persons to Christ, assuring us of the adoption of sons, leading us in our actions, purifying and sanctifying our souls and bodies, to a full and eternal enjoyment of God.[37]

The Breath of God

Mark Olson also spells out how Wesley highlighted the changes made by the Spirit, then likens the work of the Holy Spirit to breathing:

> The Spirit . . .
> *enlightens* our understanding,
> *rectifies* our will and affections,
> *renews* our nature,
> *unites* us with Christ,
> *assures* our adoption as God's children,
> *guides* our actions,
> *purifies* and *sanctifies* our souls and bodies,
> for the purpose of "full and eternal enjoyment of God."[38]

But how does the Spirit effect these changes? . . . Wesley likened the operation of the Spirit to the natural process of breathing. As the "breath of God," the Spirit inspires "every good desire" in the heart as the believer exhales back to God "unceasing love and praise and prayer." It is through this process of "spiritual respiration" that the "life of God in the soul" leavens the Christian's life.[39]

The Spirit breathes God into us, and then we exhale love, praise, and prayer back to God. This respiration brings forth the purpose and power through the Holy Spirit. To take steps in becoming more like God, we have the "means of grace," which are ways that position us to receive joy, love, and humility from the Spirit. In simple terms, the means of grace are prayer, studying the Scriptures, participating in the Lord's Supper, fasting, and Christian conferencing (gathering, fellowship). These are meant to be ways for us to be authentic and grow in our relationship with God. Let's look at each of these means of grace as opportunities for the Holy Spirit to connect with us.

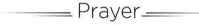

Prayer

Wesley called prayer the chief means of grace and the most important way to be in relationship with God and allow the Holy Spirit to work through us.[40] Like John Wesley, we can be people of prayer. Wesley began his day with prayer, and he closed his day with prayer. Prayer opens the door to the Holy Spirit so that God can continually empower us for service. Prayer can remove any and all possible interferences between us and God. Prayer helps us position ourselves so that we can listen for the promptings of the Holy Spirit. As E. Stanley Jones said, "Prayer is not only the refuge of the weak; it is the reinforcement of the strong."[41]

Prayer is the doorway through which the Holy Spirit enters the human heart. It's how we recognize the power of the Spirit; it's how we hear the whispers of the Spirit. Prayer can be simple. When you think of someone, offer them up in prayer. When you see joy, offer praise to God. When you see pain, present it to God.

Charles Spurgeon said, "Short prayers are long enough . . . not length but strength."[42] In his book *The Wolf at Twilight*, author Kent Nerburn relates the life of an elder of a tribe in the Dakotas who offers this: "You've got to be praying all the time or you're just thinking about yourself."[43] Make prayer an integral part of your life.

Bible Study

John Wesley wanted to be known as the "man of one book,"[44] that book being the Bible. Jesus says in John 14:26 that the Holy Spirit will teach us, and that certainly is the case when reading Scripture. Studying Scripture is a means of grace that is meant to guide us and call to mind the teachings of Jesus. "All Scripture is God-breathed and is useful for teaching, rebuking, correcting and training in righteousness, so that the servant of God may be thoroughly equipped for every good work" (2 Timothy 3:16-17, NIV).

Do you find Scripture difficult to understand? While there are many online resources to help us understand Scripture, as with anything else that comes from the internet, use discernment. One book to get you started is *What Is the Bible and Who Is It For?* by Rev. Dr. Emanuel Cleaver III.[45] This book offers an easy-to-understand explanation of the origins and purposes of the Bible for beginners. The YouVersion Bible app is one of many and not only includes multiple versions of the Bible but has tons of studies to help us understand God's Word. I use this app on my cell phone, and it is now the main way I read and study the Bible. However it works for you, make Scripture study a part of your day.

The Lord's Supper

The Lord's Supper, also referred to as Communion and the Eucharist, is a reminder of Jesus's life and teaching and a celebration of the presence of God with us. It is what we in The United Methodist Church call a sacrament, something holy, and is a way for us to participate in God's life as a community of faithful believers. During Communion, we experience a foretaste of God's kingdom and invite the Spirit within us, both individually and as a church.

John Wesley urged Methodists to partake of the Lord's Supper as often as possible. In his sermon "The Duty of Constant Communion," he says, "The grace of God given herein confirms to us the pardon of our sins by enabling us to leave them. As our bodies are strengthened by bread and wine, so are our souls by these tokens of the body and blood of Christ."[46]

The Spirit works through the Lord's Supper as an outward sign to convey an inward grace deep within our souls. This is one reason Wesley advocated for "open Communion," inviting all Christians to participate. Wesley maintained that faith was necessary, but "the full assurance of faith" was not required to receive Communion. It is an important way to feed our souls and open a door for the Spirit.

Fasting

Fasting, or "abstinence," as Wesley sometimes called it, also can connect us with God and with others. Fasting increases our awareness of our need for God and, likewise, makes us aware of the needs of others. Writer Emily Snell emphasizes that Wesley believed fasting should always be connected with prayer.[47] Fasting is also an opportunity to focus outward. For example, use the money you would have spent on food to help worthy ministries.

Steve Manskar says:

> Fasting is a powerful means of grace and the most neglected. It is powerful because fasting is a physical self-emptying that connects us with Christ (Philippians 2:7) and opens our hearts to his grace. Fasting is neglected for at least one very good reason: people are naturally reluctant to voluntarily refrain from eating. No one wants to go hungry. Especially when we are bombarded by messages at all times of the day to eat and drink. This is, I think, all the more reason for followers of Jesus Christ to practice fasting.[48]

Some skip a meal; some will go without eating for twenty-four hours. Wesley fasted weekly, from sundown Thursday to sundown Friday, only taking water and tea. The purpose of this means of grace is to open our hearts and focus our awareness on the Spirit. However, please know that some persons cannot and should not fast, for health reasons. And some persons are prone to eating disorders. The point with fasting is not really to go without but to learn to depend on God more.

═══ Christian Conferencing ═══

For early Methodists, Christian conferencing was about spiritual formation. It was a means to encourage people to serve and follow Jesus faithfully. Wesley understood that people need the larger faith community. But in-depth Christian formation happens best in small groups even today, because that is where most people feel comfortable sharing the details of their triumphs and struggles.

Christianity is meant for more than for us individually. Wesley realized that people need the support and correction of others—accountability. Find a church, Bible study, small group, or a close friend to meet you for coffee and sharing. We are all better when we share our journey with others. It's another way to breathe in the Holy Spirit and breathe back love, prayers, and praise. When we come together as the body of Christ, even when we disagree or are in conflict, the Holy Spirit is present, encouraging us to serve in one accord.

My prayer to close this chapter is a song that I've grown to love for its strength in simplicity—"Love God, Love People" by Danny Gokey.[49] As the lyrics say:

> It all comes down to this
> Love God and love people

Reflection Questions

1. What resonates with you about Wesley's journey? What surprises you?

2. Can you share a time when you gave or received joy, love, or humility?

3. How would you describe prevenient grace to another person?

4. In which of the "means of grace" do you participate? How can you grow in your participation?

5. What does Communion mean to you?

6. Why is prayer so important? Where have you seen prayer make a difference?

WIND AND GIFTS OF THE HOLY SPIRIT

We have different gifts, according to the grace given to each of us. If your gift is prophesying, then prophesy in accordance with your faith.

—Romans 12:6, NIV

What is the first thing that comes to your mind when you hear the word *gift*? Maybe you think of a present, like a Christmas gift. As preacher's kids, we received our gifts after the Christmas Eve service. We'd squirm through the program, then have to wait until Dad shook everyone's hand, gave everyone their holiday greetings, and cleaned up after the service. Then, after two eternities, he'd come home and we'd open our gifts. One year, my older brother said to me, "You know there's no Santa; it's Mom who puts out the presents." So that fateful Christmas, Mom told us to head over to the church and she'd be there in a couple of minutes. When we got outside, my brother grabbed me by the scruff of my parka and made me look through the gap in the drapes. Well, you can imagine my disappointment to see "Santa" through the curtains. Moral of the story—never have an older brother.

Maybe you think of a financial gift. Having been in fundraising for more than twenty years, I've been part of some spectacular, transformational gifts. Here are my most memorable gifts:

- I met with a woman who lived in a very modest home. She noticed I was chilly in her house, so she explained that she had decided to turn her heat down that winter, so that she'd be able to donate more to missions.

- We were in Haiti during the big earthquake in 2010. We were safe; we just didn't have a definite way to get home. A local Haitian man came and pulled me aside. He said if we needed food, he would bring some from his house. We had more food in our kitchen than he and his five kids would eat in three months. Yet, he offered us a gift beyond measure.

- A weekend before one of our Haiti trips, our then seven-year-old granddaughter and four-year-old grandson gave us a small drawstring bag. Inside the bag was some cash; they wanted to help pay for our next trip. We asked if we could give the money to kids or buy something for people in Haiti. No, they wanted us to have the money, to help us, and they gave us $1.43 to help with our costs. I think I counted correctly; it's hard to count change with tears in your eyes.

Moral of these stories—gifts come in different forms, and we determine the value.

Maybe the gift you think of is something special you are able to do—play the piano, excel in sports, speak eloquently, or do math in your head. You may have worked hard at your skill, but you also have a natural ability or gift. Moral of the story—there are gifts you may or may not know that you have.

Have you considered the gifts of the Holy Spirit? The Spirit dwells within us and has endowed us with one or more spiritual gifts. There are some variations in different traditions, but a listing of spiritual gifts in 1 Corinthians 12 includes: wisdom, knowledge, faith, healing, miracles, prophecy, discerning of spirits, speaking in tongues, and interpretation of tongues.

> Now to each one the manifestation of the Spirit is given for the common good. To one there is given through the Spirit a message of wisdom, to another a message of knowledge by means of the same Spirit, to another faith by the same Spirit, to another gifts of healing by that one Spirit, to another miraculous powers, to another prophecy, to another distinguishing between spirits, to another speaking in different kinds of tongues, and to still another the interpretation of tongues. All these are the work of one and the same Spirit, and he distributes them to each one, just as he determines. (1 Corinthians 12:7-11, NIV)

—— Extraordinary Gifts ——

"It is the Holy Spirit who moves back and forth, bringing communication from our hearts to God and from God's heart to us," wrote pastor and evangelist Lester Sumrall.[50] Sumrall also taught that *charisma* means "spiritual gift." It is an extraordinary ability that the Holy Spirit bestows on us to help us serve the body of Christ.

John Wesley referred to these as extraordinary gifts, but he cautioned that some may have been given a gift to serve a specific purpose at a particular time. "Some of them, particularly the gift of casting out evil and speaking with new tongues, appear to have been designed chiefly to convince Jews and heathens of the power and validity of the gospel."[51] Wesley also believed that some of the extraordinary gifts may have been for specific purposes in the early church and were later withdrawn. Yet, there is no doubt that Wesley believed strongly in the gifts of the Holy Spirit and the power of the Spirit working in one's life.

Sumrall, in his book *The Gifts and Ministries of the Holy Spirit*, groups the gifts of the Holy Spirit into three categories: Revelation Gifts (wisdom, knowledge, discerning of spirits); Power Gifts (faith, healing, miracles); and Inspiration Gifts (prophecy, speaking in tongues, interpretation of tongues).[52] As we look at these gifts, remember that each of us has been entrusted with one or more of them. When we actively seek them, they are revealed to us from God through the Holy Spirit.

Revelation Gifts: Wisdom, Knowledge, Discerning of Spirits

Revelation gifts are ways that God reveals information to us: information we could not come up with or conceive of on our own.

The Gift of Wisdom. This helps us make choices and give leadership that is according to God's will.

> We do, however, speak a message of wisdom among the mature, but not the wisdom of this age or of the rulers of this age, who are coming to nothing. No, we declare God's wisdom, a mystery that has been hidden and that God destined for our glory before time began. (1 Corinthians 2:6-7, NIV)

Sumrall cautions us, however, to "remember, this is not just the gift of wisdom; it is the *word* of wisdom. It is a fragment of the total wisdom of God, just as a word is a fragment of a sentence. The word of wisdom is a part or portion of the great omniscience of God."[53] Remember that God knows all; we are not gifted with knowing all but knowing some.

According to the website of The United Methodist Church, the gift of wisdom enables people to have a greater understanding of what they have learned and to use all that they know and experience to solve problems in their everyday lives. "Wise, gifted individuals make connections and help others make them as well—to understand the implications of our beliefs and actions. Those gifted with wisdom often understand root causes of disagreements, conflict, and barriers to growth and development. People with wisdom help others understand and clarify options to make good decisions."[54]

In my work as a chaplain, I've been grateful to the Spirit for the right word at the right time. Much of our work is listening and doing our best to reflect God back to the patient or family. What do you say when someone has a massive stroke, asks for prayer, receives life-threatening injuries from an accident, has made the decision to move to hospice, or dies while you are with them? The Spirit of the Lord has given me the right word too many times to count.

The Gift of Knowledge. This gift enables people to have a comprehensive understanding of a spiritual issue or circumstance. The apostle Paul wrote, "I myself am convinced, my brothers and sisters, that you yourselves are full of goodness, filled with knowledge and competent to instruct one another" (Romans 15:14, NIV).

Sophia (wisdom) is the wise application of knowledge. The gift of knowledge requires knowing God and knowing about life outside the comforts of your home. It is an understanding of the things of this world and rooting our decisions in God's Word as a foundation.

The following story dramatically demonstrates the gift of knowledge—understanding the situation, what to do in the moment, and then responding to the Holy Spirit, allowing God's love to rush through others.

~

I was teaching a course called "Death, Dying, Living, and Life after Death" at a university. It was my experience and observation that college students do not deal very well with death and dying, largely because most haven't had as much experience as many adults. The focus of the course was to provide context and resources when we experience death.

The topic for the day was the death of children. Within a few minutes of the opening of the lecture and a review of resource material, a young lady in the back said, almost shouting, "Do you know what it is like to lose a baby?" No, I don't. "Then let me tell you."

She was in the U.S. Air Force. Her pregnancy had been progressing normally, but the medical staff had used her prenatal visits as opportunities to pour out guilt and embarrassment for being single and pregnant. As she was nearing full-term, she felt a change and knew something was wrong. The baby had strangled itself on the umbilical cord. When it came time for the delivery, she asked if she could see her baby. The medical staff said, "No, you do not want to see it." But she insisted. The baby was delivered, and the attending doctor held up the baby and said, "You wanted to see the damn thing? Here it is!" It was not a pleasant experience, but she wanted and needed to see her baby.

Everyone in class gasped at the cruelty and inhumanity.

This young woman could not speak of the doctor without painting the air blue with curse words.

I asked what name she had given to her baby.

"Michelle," she said.

"Was there any kind of service for Michelle?" I asked.

"No," she said under her breath, followed by another streak of curse words.

The class gathered around her, and I offered a prayer for this woman and commended Michelle into the love and care of God. The class was dismissed, with tears flowing from the biggest football player to the meekest person in the room.

This is my most vivid experience of hearing the whisper of the Holy Spirit and following the Spirit's direction. Of knowing, then acting to do the right thing at the right time. It was an incredibly holy moment, where the presence of God was real and present.

That day my classroom was a holy and living sanctuary equal to any cathedral.

—BAB

The Gift of Discerning of Spirits. This gift helps us recognize whether or not something is truly from God or in accordance with righteousness.

> Dear friends, do not believe every spirit, but test the spirits to see whether they are from God, because many false prophets have gone out into the world. (1 John 4:1, NIV)

In this time of social media, fake news, and other warped and biased perspectives, we especially need those who have the gift of discernment—persons who can lead us to deeper understanding of God's purposes for our lives and keep us on the Holy Spirit's path. A person gifted with discernment is instinctively aware of good or bad in a given situation. He or she can separate the truth from a lie and can tell whether or not someone can be trusted. You could say that a discerning individual is "tuned in."

A friend shares her story of discerning the winds of the Holy Spirit.

We experience grief because we love deeply. Fifteen months ago, my dear husband passed. Since his death, I've made daily visits to his columbarium sight. Many days I spent my time there talking to him and weeping.

One day I stopped by for my visit, and I heard a voice say, "Don't pray to him [my late husband]; pray to Me." I instantly knew it was the Holy Spirit speaking to me. From that time forward, I not only give thanks for my husband and our fifty-three years together, but I am also grateful and give thanks for each day, for everything and everybody I've had in my life. My grief was and is still with me, but my joy has returned.

The Holy Spirit is real and walks with us through all sorts of life's journeys. I'm thankful I had that encounter and was able to discern it was the Spirit speaking directly to me.

—JQ

Power Gifts: Faith, Healing, Miracles

Power gifts allow us to glimpse the divine power of God to change human situations and outcomes. They are gifts shared with or for others.

The Gift of Faith. This is the gift to trust God and inspire others to trust God, no matter what.

> For it is by grace you have been saved, through faith—and
> this is not from yourselves, it is the gift of God—not by
> works, so that no one can boast. (Ephesians 2:8-9, NIV)

The gift of faith is more than "saving faith," which is belief in Jesus Christ and accepting him into our hearts. It's beyond being saved, a conversion experience, or justifying grace. With this gift, people know that God works in all things, that God is infinitely good, and that the people of God can rise above any hurdle. People with the gift of faith have a deep conviction that regardless of what we see with our eyes, we can trust the promises of God.

When I think of the gift of faith, my grandfather instantly comes to mind. Grandpa Blumer was a simple man with strong convictions.

Grandpa had trouble with his leg, associated with an unfortunate rendezvous with a bull. When he'd drive his old Chevy pickup down the road, he would place a two-by-four on the gas pedal, braced against the seat—an adapted cruise control. He'd take us kids on tractor rides and let us shoot his .22 rifle at pigeons in the barn or bottles on the fence. He was a serious, hardworking man who had a soft spot for his grandchildren.

The painting titled *Grace* hung over the kitchen table. It's a picture of a man with prayerful hands against his forehead; and on the table is a Bible, with folded reading glasses, a bowl with a spoon in broth, a knife, and a cut loaf of bread. It is stark in its simplicity. Minus the beard, the man in the painting encapsulates Grandpa Blumer.

Grandpa was a devout man who always had a Bible nearby. Every family gathering and every decision on the farm began with scripture

and a prayer. Grandpa would often engage the pastor in his interpretation of the scripture after worship. He and my dad would have
heated theological discussions. Grandpa did prison visits right up
to the time of his death in his nineties. But Grandpa's faith left no
doubts that God was in all things, that the Bible could provide the
answers to all our questions, and with faith, God could help us overcome any obstacle. Grandpa exemplified the gift of faith.

The Gift of Healing. This wondrous gift enables a person to use
God's healing power to cure ills and alleviate suffering.

> Is anyone among you sick? Let them call the elders of the
> church to pray over them and anoint them with oil in the
> name of the Lord. And the prayer offered in faith will make
> the sick person well; the Lord will raise them up. If they
> have sinned, they will be forgiven. (James 5:14-15, NIV)

Healing is a complex process. It takes caring persons walking
alongside those with medical knowledge. Healers are moved to be
with those who are suffering. Healers pray for, pray with, and visit
the ill. They are able to channel God's healing love to aid and comfort those in need.

Our role is to channel God's love to those who suffer different
kinds of pain. Our obligation is to pray for and walk alongside those
who are in need of healing. Most chaplains wrestle with the gifts of
healing. Why do some persons have more than their share of sick-
ness? Why do the good and faithful suffer? Why do some receive
miraculous cures while others seem to be denied?

Michael Koulianos, in his book *Holy Spirit: The One Who Makes
Jesus Real*, testifies to personal healing stories.[55] His father contracted
a rare disease that attacked the tissue and bone in his knee. A priest

touched his dad, electricity filled the room, and Koulianos wrote about how the Holy Spirit healed his dad, who was immediately able to throw away his wheelchair and crutches.

Michael himself also experienced healing through a pastor who called him to the altar. Wave after wave of power coursed through his body, and all the symptoms of the Epstein-Barr virus instantly went away. His book goes on to encapsulate the incredible healing powers he has found through the Holy Spirit.

You may be thinking, *Are these stories even real?* The following is a story from a colleague that shows healing through prayer.

Ten years ago, my wife, Cindy, was diagnosed with stage 4 neck cancer, two days before Thanksgiving. It weighed heavily on our minds to wait until after Thanksgiving to share the diagnosis with our family. The holiday season is a tough time to deliver and receive this kind of news.

Cindy and I were at the doctor's office the very next week to hear the cancer treatment plan. We were confident in our doctors, as they are some of the best, but we still had no idea what the future would hold.

Within a week they were moving ahead, as they said that being aggressive was important. The first surgery was to place the feeding tube and chemo port, and they explained how they were to be used and kept clean. A neck mold had to be made for the radiation treatment. Radiation and chemotherapy were started in the next couple of weeks. We found out how important the feeding tube would be, as she was unable to swallow food. Cindy needed the nourishment, as she lost thirty pounds in the next five months—making a thin woman even thinner. The chemo and radiation were working; she just needed sustenance and to stay hydrated.

After five months, the chemo and radiation regimen was completed, and we went back to see our physician. The doctor said that the big lump on her neck had become smaller, but surgery was necessary to remove the tumor. Surgery was scheduled the following Saturday.

While waiting for the surgeon in the pre-operating room, we said a prayer. Cindy and I have always been a prayerful family. We also spent time in prayer with our children when they were at home. The doctor came into the room and, of course, had to summarize all of the things that could go wrong and possible side effects. None of them sounded good. There are a lot of nerves and muscles in this part of the neck. Also, if surgery wasn't done within a two-month time frame, the lump could attach itself to the carotid artery and an operation wouldn't even be possible.

The doctor left to get ready for the surgery. Cindy and I said another prayer for healing and that God's will be done. The doctor used a marker to circle the spot where the lump was to be removed. Cindy was taken to surgery, and I waited in the guest waiting area. Fifteen minutes later the doctor came to the waiting area. It was not hard to find me, as it was Saturday, and I was the only one there.

I was very worried because the doctor asked me to follow him to the consult room. This surgery was to take four to five hours, so this just did not feel good. The doctor reassured me that it was not bad news.

While he had Cindy on the operating table and ready to start surgery, he could not find the lump. He looked at the area of the neck he had marked but also felt all around that side of the neck. There was no lump. I asked how this was possible. The doctor looked at me and said, "It could only have been through the power of prayer." He said that as soon as Cindy was ready, we could go home. There was nothing more to be done but to say "Praise the Lord" for this unexplained healing through the power of the Holy Spirit.

—Chuck and Cindy

I have asked my colleague to pray for me if I ever need surgery!

The Gift of Miracles. This is the gift to see signs and miracles that give credibility to God's Word and the gospel message.

> God did extraordinary miracles through Paul, so that even handkerchiefs and aprons that had touched him were taken to the sick, and their illnesses were cured and the evil spirits left them. (Acts 19:11-12, NIV)

"Those with the spiritual gift of miracles often have a heightened sensitivity to the presence and power of God through [the] Holy Spirit."[56] They believe without hesitation that God is always with us and that God is powerful, and they share this vision with others, so others will have that same certainty. The gift of miracles is not always about "miracles" as we think of them; that is, involving some extraordinary, "miraculous" event. Those having this gift can see miracles in ordinary, day-to-day situations.

My story started when I was in college and began to feel sick. I made it to my hometown doctor, who said that I would need to go to Omaha that night—not tomorrow—that night. I was diagnosed with a rare cancer, and after surgery we met Dr. S, a pathologist and oncologist.

My treatments were brutal. Chemotherapy alternated between two experimental medicines. One treatment was five days; then I'd have a couple of weeks off and, if my white blood count was high enough, the next treatment was for three days. There were times when no family could visit because my immunity was so low. The main thing I remember about chemo is they started bringing a larger garbage can for me to throw up in. I developed open sores in my mouth. I felt miserable all the time. This lasted for over a year.

We were a young couple, with a baby on the way, and I was only able to work sporadically. I had an extremely supportive boss, who let me work when I could and understood when I wasn't able. It was concrete construction work, so at times I was just too weak.

Dr. S told my wife that I had six months to a year, at the most. For sure, we'd never have any more children due to the strength of the chemo. Days grew into weeks into months in the hospital. There were too many tests, blood samples, CAT scans, and procedures to remember. For ten years of my life, I received some kind of treatment or attended scheduled checkups.

Along this journey, there were so many caring people,

so many "angels." The hospital cleaning lady came in to talk to me, watch TV; she'd even drink my coffee so I'd get liquid consumption credit. When my wife and new son came to visit, the nurses would take my son and show him around, so we could spend time together as a couple. Family members snuck food into the hospital. A social worker advocated for this young, penniless couple to save us from financial ruin. So many people prayed for us.

But Dr. S stands out above the rest. When the chemo ended, the appointments continued. I still had to come for three-month testing that eventually stretched to six months. He'd do caring things for us, like give us passes to the zoo, to enjoy as a family. When he and his wife drove through our town on their way to see relatives, they'd stop and take us out for a steak dinner. He was not only a doctor; he became a friend.

Every year they'd invite cancer families to a huge Christmas gathering. I resisted going to these parties, but one year we decided to go. It was very emotional for me to thank Dr. S for all he did for us. It was emotional for Dr. S when we informed him that we named our second son after him (and were blessed with a third son later).

Dr. S said I was one of three "true miracles." Throughout my treatment the scans showed spots where my cancer had spread to the stomach, liver, and spleen. Then they were gone. He has no explanation other than my case was a miracle. Our only explanation is the power of prayer and the Holy Spirit.

For his eightieth birthday, Dr. S had a big birthday party in Omaha. We were invited but were reluctant to go, thinking we'd be sitting at the back of the room and not know anyone. At the head table was Dr. S, his wife, and the three miracle families. Dr. S was too modest to explain to the gathering why we were there, but my wife and I knew. For over forty years now, we've been at the head table of God's miracles.

—RT

Inspiration Gifts: Prophecy, Speaking in Tongues, Interpretation of Tongues

The first two groups—gifts of revelation and gifts of power—are gifts that have the potential to change the world. Gifts of inspiration are for the benefit of the church so the church is vibrant and reaches others.

The Gift of Prophecy. This is the gift to declare a message from God.[57]

> Follow the way of love and eagerly desire gifts of the Spirit, especially prophecy. (1 Corinthians 14:1, NIV)

"The gift of prophecy is the ability to speak God's word to others, or more appropriately to be open for God to speak God's word through us. Prophets are incisive, clear, and often controversial, communicators. Prophets see things that others often don't, and they have the courage to 'tell it like it ought to be.'"[58]

The Greek word for the gift of prophecy is *propheteia*, which is the ability to receive a divinely inspired message and deliver it to others. The Holy Spirit gives the gift of prophecy to some believers to make God's heart known.

Listen—Hear—Respond:
Sharilyn's Story

My thirty-four-year-old daughter, Jennifer, died unexpectedly of a rare autoimmune blood disorder after just eight weeks of rapidly declining health. Jennifer was spunky, caring, passionate, always busy, and had always been healthy. She loved special-needs children and spent her occupational therapy career focused on developing and supporting them and their families, mostly focused on children with autism.

When she took her last breath on this earth, Jen was surrounded by love and family. It was a few weeks after that I realized that as her mom I had been blessed to be present at both my daughter's very first breath on this earth and her last. Through the prayers of others, God's great mercy and holy presence filled the room, covered our family, and strengthened our hearts. We felt a most unexplainable peace over us through her hospitalization and passing. This gift of the Spirit's presence was a most gracious and awesome gift to our family as we walked through a most unbelievable journey.

In losing my daughter, I have experienced a deep grief; an unfillable, unique absence; and a pain in my chest that physically cuts into my heart and breath. But I also felt the very close presence of the strength and power of the Holy Spirit and have a deeper appreciation for words like *peace, grace, love, hope,* and *eternity.* I have personally experienced the words of Psalm 18:16 to be true: "He reached down from on high and took hold of me / he drew me out of deep waters" [NIV].

In the weeks and months after Jen's death, I had the overwhelming need to tell her story; more specifically, to share God's story lived through Jen's life. I am most definitely not a public speaker! In fact, speaking in front of people would be at the bottom of the list of last things I would choose to do! But the need to tell Jen's story wouldn't go away.

I started by posting on Facebook, where many of our family friends and Jen's friends had connected with me. There were many times when I had no intention or particular thoughts to share, but something would come to mind and the words showed up in that moment. I often wondered, "Where did the words come from?" And I learned quickly that the Holy Spirit supplied the words when I didn't know what to say.

But that wasn't enough. God kept nudging me that there's more I had to do. Share Jen's story. But also share about God's grace and faithfulness when we went through the "deep waters" of her illness and death. In conversation, I had told a friend about it, and she was determined that our story was a story to be shared. She arranged for me to speak at a women's group in the area. Because I am not a public speaker, I wrote up the story, entitled "Deep Waters," and simply read it to the group. The reaction was amazing.

That night led to three other speaking engagements, all of various audience sizes (twenty-five to sixty), and all very fulfilling in that people came up afterward to share their own grief journeys and relate their own grace stories. And each time, I expected that I had completed the task of sharing Jen's story, but each time the urge to share remained.

After hearing me speak at one of these events, my close friend arranged for me to speak in my hometown, where Jen had lived her growing-up years. They scheduled a room in a church that fit about seventy-five people. As people began to arrive, it soon became evident that this wasn't going to be enough space, so we had to quickly move everything into the sanctuary. We were amazed and humbled that over two hundred people showed up to hear God's story through Jen's story! It was a night of worship, sharing, connecting, and both hearing and experiencing God's great desire to be an intimate part of every part of our lives and to ultimately bring us home to God. Amazingly, after that night, the feeling of sharing with others was gone. It seemed God's ultimate intention was for me to return "home" to tell of God's love and grace to those people we knew, who lived in community with us and who connected with us.

The Holy Spirit nudges us and provides us opportunities. It doesn't have to be speaking to groups; it can be as simple as talking to a friend over a cup of coffee, answering questions of someone who wants to hear more about what God has done for you.

I still miss Jen every day. I still talk to others about her life. I still reflect on how the Holy Spirit worked through that experience. I still remain grateful to God for pushing me to share her story with others.

The Gift of Speaking in Tongues. While there are various understandings of this gift, when I use it, I am referring to a practice in which people utter words or speechlike sounds that some believe to be languages unknown to the speaker. Another word for this is *glossolalia*.

Some religious traditions find speaking in tongues integral to their belief and connection with the Holy Spirit. For example, Pentecostal churches teach that speaking in tongues is evidence that a person has received baptism by the Holy Spirit. Then there are other religious traditions that skeptically look at speaking in tongues as provocative or contrived.

In my conversations, I've found people who see speaking in tongues as a deeply spiritual experience. Others have described how the gift of tongues was integral to their baptism. There are plenty of authors who describe the same, so I am not discounting this connection with the Holy Spirit. I don't believe we need to deny believers this gift, but I also don't believe we need Holy Spirit ultimatums that if you don't have a particular experience, like speaking in tongues, you can't experience the power of God through the Holy Spirit.

For certain, the gift of tongues is controversial. As mentioned earlier in the chapter, John Wesley felt this gift may have been given for a specific purpose in the early church and later withdrawn. Wesley advised followers to "proceed with extreme caution," saying further that "God divided these gifts with a sparing hand. Even then, not all were prophets. Not all were workers of miracles. Not all had the gifts of healing. Not all spoke in tongues."[59]

Wesley was a practically minded person; however he "taught that the Holy Spirit does work wonders in one's heart and life."[60] Speaking in tongues is not a requirement of salvation or to receive the love of God. Of utmost concern for Wesley was that we engage in the means of grace, along with opening our hearts and minds to the winds and whispers of the Holy Spirit.

The Gift of Interpretation of Tongues. This gift is closely related to the gift of speaking in tongues. As the name implies, this gift gives a person the ability to interpret speaking in tongues.

> If any speak in a tongue, let there be only two or at most three, and each in turn, and let someone interpret. But if there is no one to interpret, let each of them keep silent in church and speak to himself and to God. (1 Corinthians 14:27-28)

Those with the gift of interpreting tongues are able to provide understanding by breaking down barriers. Their ability to intuitively understand others, along with the culture and context of their language, builds a bridge between the speaker and listener.

Conclusion

One of my favorite memories of preaching was in a church in Haiti. Speaking with an interpreter takes a delicate balance. You need to speak slow enough and in small enough segments to allow the translator to understand and translate, but fast enough so there is continuity and expression in the words. I also have to remember to speak in context. There are things our Haitian brothers and sisters may not have encountered or experienced. I was preaching about grace and the love of God, and I said one sentence and my translator went on in Haitian Creole for about three minutes. When he finished, I smiled and said, "Wow. I must have been great." The translator laughed. "I forgot I was speaking for you; I was speaking for God."

Can't argue with that.

Let Us Pray

Let us pray these lines from the hymn "Many Gifts, One Spirit."

> Many gifts, one Spirit, one love known in many ways. . . .
> For the Giver, for the gifts, praise, praise, praise.[61]

Reflection Questions

1. What other gifts are listed in the Bible? Compare gifts discussed in Ephesians 4:7-13, Isaiah 11:2-3, and Romans 12:3-8.

2. Do you know your spiritual gifts? Take a spiritual gifts inventory. One inventory is offered by the Board of Discipleship Ministries, The United Methodist Church: https://www.umcdiscipleship.org/spiritual-gifts-inventory/en.

3. What gifts do you feel God has revealed to you? How can you use this gift with the winds of the Holy Spirit?

4. What have you learned so far about the Holy Spirit? What questions remain?

5. Where have you seen miracles in your everyday life?

WHISPERS AND FRUIT OF THE HOLY SPIRIT

"I am the vine; you are the branches.
If you remain in me and I in you,
you will bear much fruit;
apart from me you can do nothing."

—John 15:5, NIV

Think of your favorite fruit. Crisp grapes? Fresh peaches? Bright pineapple? Juicy pears? My two favorites are mangos from Haiti, nothing sweeter, followed closely by plump blueberries—so tasty. Fruit is meant to be picked and enjoyed. It's the product of a vine or tree or bush. The sweetness is available to everyone—as long as it isn't from your neighbor's tree.

"Unlike the gifts of the Spirit, *the fruit of the Spirit is not divided among believers.* Instead, *all* Christians should be marked by *all* the fruit of the Spirit," wrote Billy Graham.[62] The good news is that unlike gifts, all the fruit are available to us. The news that should give us pause is, all the fruit are expected of us.

In the previous chapter we highlighted the gifts of the Holy Spirit. Those gifts bear witness to the winds and whispers of the Holy Spirit. These spiritual gifts are evidence of God's presence in our lives and our cooperation with God's will. Through the fruit, the Holy Spirit becomes a reality in our lives and in the lives of those we touch. If we are rooted in the Holy Spirit, these fruit inevitably appear.

John Wesley said it this way: "The Holy Spirit does more than give gifts; it produces fruit. Fruit are the outward expression of these inward gifts."[63] With God as our trunk, our base, we can bear much fruit. Apart from God we are nothing and our vines wither. Further, like edible fruit, spiritual fruit takes time to grow and ripen. Listening to God's voice, whether as a mighty gust of wind or a gentle whisper, doesn't bear fruit overnight.

Listen—Hear—Respond: The Story of LaGonave Alive!

One of the greatest gifts given to me, where the Holy Spirit has produced fruit, has been mission work in Haiti. I've said this many times: I feel God has simply put me in the right place, and I've tried to listen for the Spirit and be faithful.

My first trip to the island of La Gonâve, Haiti was in 2008. One of the last nights there, we met in a church that at the time had no roof; it was just four walls. The missionaries introduced us to an orphan, William, who had the dream of becoming a doctor. It still brings tears to my eyes when I think about us surrounding William and praying for a way to make his dream come true.

Our church found a way and began sponsoring William to attend medical school in Port-au-Prince in 2009. I led a medical team to La Gonâve in 2010, and William was part of that team. We also witnessed the devastation of the earthquake. William's medical school collapsed, and many of his teachers and fellow students were killed. If he hadn't been with our medical team, he may not have survived.

William came up with a new plan to attend medical school in

the Dominican Republic. And, again, we prayed for a way. God provided through our church and through generous donors. William had to learn a new language, Spanish, and in 2011 he started medical school in Santiago, Dominican Republic.

Due to the dramatic experiences of the earthquake and listening to the whispers of the Spirit, I went to La Gonâve by myself in 2011. I spent time traveling to villages to interview pastors, leaders, women's groups—frankly, anyone who would talk to me. I asked them a simple question, "What would be the best way we could help?" Overwhelmingly, people said they needed support in education and health care. They told me how difficult life is for women, children, and the elderly. Consequently, we've tried to stay true to these areas as our core.

We began small. We sent a handful of school scholarships, sent money to feed children and the elderly, started a Christmas program, and continued to support William in medical school. In 2013, the pastor of our church said the ministry was getting too big and we needed to start our own nonprofit.

In November 2013, LaGonave Alive officially became a 501(c)(3) nonprofit. We grew as God and funds allowed. Dr. William graduated from medical school in 2016 and returned to the island. We purchased a building and opened a clinic in the small village of Zetwa. We also began receiving food packets from Kids Against Hunger and Mercy Meals, shipped by Orphan Grain Train, which greatly enhanced our feeding programs. We started a "Back to School" program—buying pens, pencils, and notebooks for up to two thousand children in schools on La Gonâve. Many kids don't have basic school supplies or are often forced to share them with a sibling.

In 2017, we broke ground for a school. I've said many times it is better to be confidently naive than smart, and this was a prime example. We had grown in our school sponsorships, but kids were going to many different schools—some good, some not so good. We thought we could use our scholarship money and begin our own school. It was a bigger project than expected, but the Holy Spirit continued to provide wind for our efforts.

In September 2018, we dedicated the Rob Marchand Institute. Rob was my best friend who died from cancer, and it was such a blessing to have his wife and two kids there to open the school. The first level of our school was completed with five classrooms. We opened with grades 1–3 and a principal's office.

At the dedication, all I could think about was how nice the school turned out and how much hard work it took to create this school. Every inch of the foundation was dug by hand. All the concrete to form the foundation, stick the blocks together, and complete the columns and steps were mixed with shovels and sweat, carried bucket by bucket by local workers. The effort it took to complete this building was incredible.

In 2019, we added grade 4, which meant our first floor was filled, so we needed to start the second level. We also bought a school bus and transported it to the island. In 2020, we finished the second level, and our hope is to add a classroom until the building is filled.

We've done so many things to raise funds. I have donated profits from my books: *Paths, Proverbs, & Lessons from Haiti* (2011); *I Saw God Today* (2013); *Parsonage Parables* (2015); *Even a Little Raindrop* (2016)—a children's book; *Simply Grace: Everyday Glimpses of God* (2019) from GBHEM Publishing; *Turtle Bay* (2020) another children's book illustrated by a local artist; and the book you're reading will be added to this list.

We also started a monthly donor club to support William; my

wife made and sold crocheted bears, had a Block by Block fundraiser, ran an online Giving Square program, solicited student/teacher sponsors, held a Raise the Roof fundraiser, and too many more projects to remember.

I can't tell you how many times I thought, *I have no idea how we're going to pay for that!* And a check would show up. So many churches and individuals have been faithful. There have been some difficult times too. We've made some mistakes. We've had times of disappointment. We've been discouraged. In the midst of those times, we have come to know and love the people of La Gonâve, God's children, who deserve our care. I have felt the Holy Spirit move within me, team members, and our Haitian sisters and brothers. God's footprint has been all over this ministry. What does the future hold? I do not know. But I live with these two scriptures:

> Therefore do not worry about tomorrow, for tomorrow will worry about itself. Each day has enough trouble of its own. (Matthew 6:34, NIV)

and

> But as for me and my household, we will serve the LORD. (Joshua 24:15, NIV)

The Fruit of the Holy Spirit

> But the fruit of the Spirit is love, joy, peace, patience, kindness, goodness, faithfulness, gentleness, self-control. (Galatians 5:22-23)

There is but one fruit of the Holy Spirit; but, according to Galatians, it comes in these nine varieties. These nine are inseparable and overlap in our inward being. And as you grow in your relationship with

God, these fruits will become more and more apparent. As a note, in her fun article, "If the Fruit of the Spirit Were Actual Fruit," Tristen Coffee makes some interesting pairings, some of which I've borrowed below just because.[64]

The Fruit of Love

Strawberries are red, the color of love, and they grow together in bunches. Like lovers, strawberries hang close together.

The Greek language actually has four different words for love. When the New Testament talks about God's perfect, unselfish love, the writer often uses the word *agape.*

"Agape describes the deliberate effort, which we can only make with the help of God, never to seek anything but the best, even for those who seek the worst for us."[65] When we act with agape, we set aside our own preferences, desires, and sometimes even needs to put the other person first. Acting with this kind of love requires strength. Agape is not acquiescing to someone else's will for us. It is not letting someone run over us. Rather, it is being able to see the other person as God sees and act accordingly with no hidden motives or agenda.

> Therefore if you have any encouragement from being united with Christ, if any comfort from his love, if any common sharing in the Spirit, if any tenderness and compassion, then make my joy complete by being like-minded, having the same love, being one in spirit and of one mind. Do nothing out of selfish ambition or vain conceit. Rather, in humility value others above yourselves. (Philippians 2:1-3, NIV)

It was the Christmas that none of us wanted to remember.

But we all do. Not only was it Christmas, but it was also Mom and Dad's anniversary. Dad loved to surprise Mom! One year it was a new mattress that he had hidden under their bed for three months. Mom didn't even notice it was there! Another year it was a hand-carved coffee table that Dad had worked on in his office. To see Mom's face light up with joy, to feel the love between them and us at that moment . . . that for us was what Christmas was all about.

But this Christmas was different. That love between us, you see, had broken . . . been shattered.

That summer my sister Rachel (number two of our eight) had been killed in a car accident coming home from college. Ida (number one) and Gretchen (number three) were in the car with her. They had been spared but could never escape what came after—the guilt, the pain, the hopelessness. None of us could run from that. Oh, we did a pretty good job of disguising it all. We might even had been able to pretend our way through this broken Christmas, had not my brother (number five) accidentally run over our dog. No one could pretend then. The veil had been torn. The dam had broken. Grief and everything that came with it seeped into every corner of our home and hearts.

Dad, ever the pastor, tried to lead us through this valley of the shadow of death, but how do you do that when you yourself are lost? And Mom, our "holy comforter," tried to be the ever-present shoulder to cry on. But how do you do that when you have no shoulder yourself to lean on?

After the Christmas Eve candlelight service, we all milled around the dining room table. Waiting. Waiting for Dad to pull us out of this pit with his traditional surprise for Mom. We didn't care what it was; we were all just ready for something to break through this ugly scent of silence.

It wasn't to be. Dad, lost in his own grief, forgot to get Mom a gift. A tiny tear trickled down Mom's cheek. She tried to hide her disappointment, but an hour later that disappointment turned into "bread" as she announced that she had forgotten the oysters this year and instead of oyster stew (Dad's favorite) we were having potato soup!

And so, the McBride family gathered around the table; and although none of us would admit it, all eyes were fixed on that one unmentionable chair—sitting empty between Gretchen and Ida.

Suddenly, there was a knock on the door. Dad jumped up and did something he never, ever did . . . he swore! In some ways I think we all did. "Who in the blankety-blank has the blank to knock on our door on Christmas Eve! What can they possibly want now!"

As I watched Dad stomp to the door, I pondered the question that had been hovering ever since Rachel's accident: "Are we going to make it . . . Can we, as a family, survive this?" Dad opened the door, and we all silently groaned as we witnessed just who this intruder was. It was Orlando, a Native American we all knew too well. He often knocked on our door in a drunken stupor to borrow food or beg for money. We watched as Dad put on a forced smile and allowed Orlando into the darkness none of us could hide anymore. And then it happened.

It started when we all realized the smell that wasn't in the room. Orlando wasn't drunk! He stood before us sober. "Reverend," he said, "I'm sorry to interrupt, but I just wanted to come and say a prayer for you. I know you pray for so many of us. I will forever remember the prayer you said for me when I lost my son. And so, I wonder if you'd let me say a prayer for you?"

Stunned and confused, we all gathered around this strange guest. All of us, except for two (Mom and Dad) held hands. Orlando humbly removed his hat and offered a prayer, first in Lakota and then in English. And as everyone closed their eyes, I watched out of the corner of mine, as my father's hand slowly traveled across the abyss that separated us and gently brushed my mother's hand, still fisted and hard. But as the incense of that prayer began to unfold, Mom's hand did as well, and gently embraced Dad's.

Christ, Emmanuel, God with us, had come.

This strange vagabond who was incessantly in need, was now praying and showing love for me! And for each of my family! Orlando, this blessed stranger, had come bearing gifts. With the gift of prayer he had broken open this vial of love upon our feet, and its fragrance was suddenly filling the room. And with that love came hope. As I experienced that fragrance, an assurance came over me. Yes, we were broken; but somehow, I knew right then that we were going to make it through this. For I began to realize that God's love, you see, does come down. Even in the darkest and lowest of places. Even to me.

—Brook

The Fruit of Joy

What says summer and fun more than watermelon? Joy overflows just like its juiciness. Even the leftover rind reminds us of a big smile.

The Greek word *chara* is most often translated as "joy." It is the realization of God's love and grace in our lives. It is a feeling of gladness and gratefulness that we exude no matter our circumstances. While the world says that joy may be fleeting, the joy of the Lord is everlasting and pours out of us, thereby transforming our circumstances and infusing them with meaning.

> Consider it pure joy, my brothers and sisters, whenever you face trials of many kinds, because you know that the testing of your faith produces perseverance. (James 1:2-3, NIV)

In the '90s, I was doing youth ministry for a church. Part of that ministry in the summer was to take groups of junior high and senior high students to Camp Hope, to serve as counselors for people with physical and mental disabilities. On Sunday evening all the counselors went through a training period, learning how to help the various campers with whatever disability they might have.

This was a new experience for me and for many of the students who had never done anything like this previously. We were quite anxious about how we were going to interact with the campers. The campers arrived on Monday; many had previous experiences at Camp Hope and were excited to be there. We had supper together, learned our camper's names, and helped them get situated in their cabins.

We gathered at the small basketball court in the middle

of the camp for a dance. The sun was just going down and the light was golden. I remember that Beach Boys music was playing, and our students began to dance with their individual campers. Some were in wheelchairs; some were wearing helmets so they wouldn't hurt their heads, some were blind or using some kind of adaptive equipment.

As we were dancing to the music, I thought to myself, *This is what heaven must be like. All of us together, enjoying each other's company, and dancing in pure joy.*

Was the Holy Spirit there? How could the Spirit not be?

—RVB

The Fruit of Peace

Cherries have been shown to calm our nervous system and help people sleep. As a side note, it's also fun to spit the seeds.

> Rejoice in the Lord always; again I will say, Rejoice. Let your gentleness be known to everyone. The Lord is near. Do not worry about anything, but in everything by prayer and supplication with thanksgiving let your requests be made known to God. And the peace of God, which surpasses all understanding, will guard your hearts and your minds in Christ Jesus.
>
> Finally, beloved, whatever is true, whatever is honorable, whatever is just, whatever is pure, whatever is pleasing, whatever is commendable, if there is any excellence and if there is anything worthy of praise, think about these things. Keep on doing the things that you have learned and received and heard and seen in me, and the God of peace will be with you. (Philippians 4:4-9, NRSV)

Peace is knowing at your deepest level that all is well. Despite appearances to the contrary, everything is in God's hands. From the book of Philippians, we can see how to abide in God's peace. First, we celebrate who God is; and, second, we bring our worries, fears, and concerns to God in prayer.

Maybe it's because we have so much technology and we know so much more, but the world doesn't seem at peace. We can't control the world, but we can focus on our own relationship with God. It reminds me of the song "It Is Well with My Soul." The haunting melody and repetition convince us that despite what surrounds us, despite life's storms, we can be at peace. It can be well with our souls.

～

A member of our congregation was scheduled for major surgery. She was very anxious and fearful. There were two factors that contributed to the deep feelings. She was a person of great faith and felt guilty about her fear. And she was a nurse. It is my observation nurses know the possible complications of medical procedures and that knowledge brings fear.

The night before the surgery, I met with the family and shared Communion with them. As I was about to leave, I stepped to the bedside to give her a blessing and benediction. I could see the lines in her face of fear and anxiety fading away, and a glow appeared in her eyes. A beautiful smile emerged, and she said, "I will be all right. I'm at peace." It was a special moment of hearing whispers of peace through the Holy Spirit through the bread and the cup.

—BAB

The Fruit of Patience

Patience and pomegranates go together, because pomegranates take forever to take apart and eat.

The word for patience in Greek actually translates most closely to a word we don't commonly use—"forbearance." Forbearance is refraining from something. It includes patience but also endurance, constancy, steadfastness, perseverance, long-suffering, and slowness in avenging wrongs. The fruit of patience enables us to endure and withstand challenging situations.

> "Be completely humble and gentle; be patient, bearing with
> one another in love." (Ephesians 4:2, NIV)

In my almost twenty years of nursing, the Holy Spirit has often been present in my work. There are times I know the Spirit has put me in a particular place or time for the good of another individual.

One incident that stands out was when I met an incredibly special patient and his wife. Even though it happened years ago, I vividly remember the four months that I cared for them. I was drawn to this tall man with an even bigger personality from the moment I welcomed him onto the unit and settled him in his room. Over the first few weeks that I cared for him, he entertained me with his humor and the stories he told from his life. He was about my father's age, and although I knew he had children from a previous marriage, he rarely talked about them in the beginning. I could tell he had regrets and hurt feelings from his past, but it would not be until the last few weeks of his life that I truly understood why.

As one month turned into two and three, and after several setbacks, we settled into a routine each shift I was with him. I knew when to push him to do more and when to let him rest and, most importantly, when he needed to talk. Going through a blood and marrow transplant when you only have your wife for support is scary, lonely, and inevitably makes one reflect on life and relationships. It was during his last month that he shared his heartache that his relationship with his daughters had suffered after his marriage failed. This man, who was now a cherished friend, wanted his daughters to understand the decisions he had made but was afraid they would not listen. This is when I knew that the Holy Spirit had crossed our paths for my benefit as much as his.

My father and I had a strained relationship as a result of his infidelity and lack of involvement in my sister's and my life. I was in my midtwenties, finding my way in the world and reexamining relationships that had caused heartache, when this particular man came into my life. I could see so much of my own relationship with my father in his relationship with his daughters. The feelings he shared with me were everything I had wanted my father to share with me. Eventually he did have the opportunity to connect with each of his daughters, and although he did not survive his transplant, he left this world knowing that his girls had forgiven him and had a better understanding of his perspective.

I grieved my own loss of this man and shared the family's heartache as they said their goodbyes. I am forever grateful for this time and the lessons he taught me. Our late-night conversations have stayed with me over the years and continue to guide me as I navigate my relationship with my own father. Although I will never completely understand the decisions my father has made, my special patient reminds me that my own father is hurting and wishing for more. Had the Holy Spirit not crossed our paths, I am fairly certain I would not have continued to work on my relationship with my father, and my children would have missed out on knowing their grandfather.

—Bobbie

The Fruit of Kindness

When I think about kindness, I am reminded of coconuts. A coconut can be used in many ways—as a drinking cup, a musical instrument, and so on. Likewise, kindness can be of benefit in many different kinds of situations.

Closely related, and sometimes translated as goodness, kindness conveys a generosity of spirit. When we think of someone who is kind, we tend to think of someone who is good and tolerant. What is more useful than just showing kindness to others? What deescalates anger? Kindness. What brings a smile to someone in need? Kindness. What can the world never get enough of? Kindness.

> Or do you show contempt for the riches of his kindness, forbearance and patience, not realizing that God's kindness is intended to lead you to repentance? (Romans 2:4, NIV)

One evening I was sitting at a table, drinking coffee at my favorite place and reading a book. As I sat there, I heard a nudge in my spirit: "*Go to the Gospel Mission!*"

"What?"

It came a second time: "*Go to the Gospel Mission!*"

I looked at my watch; it was 7:40 p.m. The mission's worship service began at 8:00. I put my book in my backpack, picked up my coffee, left the store, and drove to the Gospel Mission. Upon entering the mission an outreach team from a local university was handing out song sheets for the service. I took a seat in the next-to-last pew.

It wasn't long, and I felt a tap on my shoulder. An employee asked if I would move up, because they liked to save the back pews for the women and children. I moved up to the third row. In the pew ahead of me sat an older homeless man just to my right. Soon a younger homeless man sat in front of me just to my left, leaving a space between them. I could tell they did not know each other.

The service unfolded with the worship team leading us with camp-type songs, prayer, and a brief message. When it came time to receive the offering, the worship leader prayed, and the plates began to be passed. The mission always provides an opportunity to give.

Waiting for the plate I watched as the younger man reached into his pocket and pulled out some papers. Some were notes that he put back into his pocket. He then unfolded two one-dollar bills and handed one of them to the older man. The man looked, hesitated, and then took the bill. When the offering plate came to them, they both gave.

For me, this was a modern example of the story of the woman at the temple who gave her two coins, all she had. The Holy Spirit sent me to the Gospel Mission to see kindness and present me with a question: Am I willing to show kindness and give to another, so they too have something to give?

—Roy C.

The Fruit of Goodness

An orange is brightly colored and full of vitamin C. Like goodness, an orange is full of what we need to live a healthy life.

Others can see goodness through our actions. As we deepen our relationship with the Holy Spirit, we grow in our desire to show that to others. The way we show kindness is through acts of goodness.

> With this in mind, we constantly pray for you, that our God may make you worthy of his calling, and that by his power he may bring to fruition your every desire for goodness and your every deed prompted by faith. (2 Thessalonians 1:11, NIV)

It was supposed to be just another week of church in the park. Our team set up the sound system, prayed together, and had a short worship team rehearsal before a few dozen people from our church gathered in the park for worship. As the gathering went on, I noticed a young man sitting off in the distance on a park bench. He was wearing a red baseball cap pulled down, covering his forehead. During the service, I shared a brief message out of John 14 and noticed that he was listening intently to every single word.

After the gathering, our team began the process of tearing everything down and packing up to go home when someone from our church approached this young man and began a conversation with him. After a few minutes, the person from our church introduced me to the young man. He extended his hand toward mine and said, "Hey, I'm Trenton."

We talked for a few minutes, and I soon learned that Trenton was homeless. He had spent the past several months sleeping in a tent in the back corner of the park behind trees. Not only was Trenton homeless, but he found himself in the middle of a battle with addiction to heroin and prescription drugs—a battle that had caused him to lose custody of his two young children and his marriage to his high-school sweetheart.

"I'm so lost, tired, and empty," Trenton said with tears streaming down his face. I listened to him share the story of his journey the past several months, and then I felt prompted to ask him if he had any connection with someone who loved him. "My mom," he said. I asked him where his mom lived, and he said, "Outside of Atlanta." I asked him how long it had been since they had talked, and he told me it had been a few weeks because he didn't have a phone.

So, I pulled out my phone, and he dialed a phone number with a 755 area code. Seconds later, his mom was on the other end. They both started to cry when they heard each other's voices. After talking with his mom for a few minutes, Trenton handed me the phone, and I told her that we were going to help Trenton get home to her. She explained to me through tears that she had been so worried and had been praying that the Lord would send someone to help, that the Lord would cause someone to notice him and to help carry him home. "I think that might be me," I said.

That night was the last night Trenton spent sleeping in

the park. The next morning, we picked him up with a few bagels from a local bagel shop, gave him a duffel bag filled with Gatorade, snacks, and a Bible, and then we helped him get on a bus to Georgia.

The following day his mom called me telling me how thankful she was to look at her son in the eye and wrap her arms around him again. "I thought I had laid eyes on him for the last time before you called," she said. She asked me if she could repay me in some way for the kindness that we showed him, but I told her that I wasn't interested in that. Instead, I told her that when she has an opportunity to help someone in their time of need, do it, and to just consider paying forward the goodness the Spirit had made possible that night in the park.

"We belong to each other," I said. She burst into tears on the phone and said, "I just don't know what to say to you; people don't do this kind of thing." I waited for a few seconds, listening to her cry over the phone, and said softly, "No, people don't do this kind of thing, but the Holy Spirit most definitely does."

—Dave

The Fruit of Faithfulness

In our everyday language we say that "an apple a day keeps the doctor away" and that "the apple doesn't fall far from the tree." These phrases also describe consistency and faithfulness.

Faithfulness is evidence of the Holy Spirit's work in our lives helping us, encouraging us to be dependable, trustworthy, and loyal to God and God's purposes. How do we demonstrate our reliability and obedience to the Spirit when we encounter such messages as

"Do what you like" or "Do whatever feels good" or "It's about me"? By calling on God and asking God to help us remain faithful.

> Therefore, among God's churches we boast about your perseverance and faith in all the persecutions and trials you are enduring. (2 Thessalonians 1:4, NIV)

My husband was extremely ill, and at a certain point, he was in the isolation ward of the hospital. Recovery looked very bleak, and that night, as we were in his hospital room, he whispered, "We need a miracle."

I had been thinking that, but when he said it, it became real. I grabbed my Bible and headed for a gentle spot. I prayed "O God, we need a miracle." I opened my Bible to Romans 8:26-29. "The Holy Spirit helps us in our weakness. All things work together for good for those who are called according to His purpose" [paraphrased]. I read it over and over, letting the truth sink in.

God had brought us together as a couple; I saw God's hand in our lives from way back. I saw God's faithfulness and provision in our lives throughout the past; and, in looking back, I felt strength in knowing God wouldn't leave us. I didn't know what the outcome was going to be, but I had great peace in knowing we were in God's hands.

Then I turned a few pages back in my Bible and landed on Romans 5:2. "Because of our faith, Christ has brought us into this place of UNDESERVED PRIVILEGE" (NLT, emphasis added). Then I saw in my mind an open door, and I heard a voice saying, "Come here, my child." In my mind, and in my prayer, I walked through that open door, prayed to the Almighty, and asked for a miracle. I cannot begin to describe the peace I had as I went back to my husband's room, still not knowing the outcome, but to remain faithful as we are in God's hands. God, through the Holy Spirit, gave us the miracle we were hoping for!

—Ramona

The Fruit of Gentleness

Banana—handle with care or it will bruise.

Gentleness, like humility, is a sign of God's grace in our soul. It is not weakness. Rather, gentleness is strength under control. As a gentle horse accepts the rein of the rider, so gentle people trust God and accept God's guidance. Strength in our convictions can be shown in how we care for others, how we reach out with care and compassion.

> "Take my yoke upon you and learn from me, for I am gentle and humble in heart, and you will find rest for your souls." (Matthew 11:29, NIV)

Mother Teresa once said, "Be kind to each other. It is better to commit faults with gentleness than to work miracles with unkindness."[66]

The Fruit of Self-Control

Grapefruit and self-control go together. With grapefruit, we set aside the bitterness and sourness to taste the sweet.

Self-control is the ability to regulate one's emotions, thoughts, and behavior despite being confronted by temptation and impulses that try to take us in another direction. Self-control gives us the power to say yes to the Spirit and those things that are good for us, and no to those things that are not of God. Self-control fosters a beautiful, bountiful harvest of spiritual fruit. Yet, when we talk about *self*-control, we really mean that we put our *self* into God's hands and, as the song says, let Jesus "take the wheel."[67] We derive sweetness of the Holy Spirit by setting aside the sourness of temptation, indulgence, and instant gratification.

> For the Spirit God gave us does not make us timid, but gives us power, love and self-discipline. (2 Timothy 1:7, NIV)

To illustrate kindness and self-control, here is a story from John 8:1-11 (*The Message*).

> Jesus went across to Mount Olives, but he was soon back in the Temple again. Swarms of people came to him. He sat down and taught them.
>
> The religion scholars and Pharisees led in a woman who had been caught in an act of adultery. They stood her in plain sight of everyone and said, "Teacher, this woman was caught red-handed in the act of adultery. Moses, in the Law, gives orders to stone such persons. What do you say?" They were trying to trap him into saying something incriminating so they could bring charges against him.
>
> Jesus bent down and wrote with his finger in the dirt. They kept at him, badgering him. He straightened up and said, "The sinless one among you, go first: Throw the stone." Bending down again, he wrote some more in the dirt.
>
> Hearing that, they walked away, one after another, beginning with the oldest. The woman was left alone. Jesus stood up and spoke to her. "Woman, where are they? Does no one condemn you?"
>
> "No one, Master."
>
> "Neither do I," said Jesus. "Go on your way. From now on, don't sin."

First of all, don't you wonder what he wrote in the dirt? Maybe Jesus was just diverting his attention away. Or maybe he wrote, "Gotcha!" Probably not. Regardless, Jesus showed his gentleness to the woman and self-control with the scholars and Pharisees, while teaching us all a lesson about recognizing that we all sin and fall short of the glory of God.

Conclusion

Fruit is edible food, but the word also refers to the action or result of hard work; for example, the fruit of our labors. The result of the hard work of the Spirit is the fruit of the Spirit *in us*—the evidence of the Holy Spirit's work in our lives. Jesus's words, "I am the vine; you are the branches" (John 15:5), speak to the close relationship between who we can be, how we can act, and the Spirit— the closer we are to God, the more abundant is the fruit we have to share.

Clinical pastoral education, the coursework and experiential learning to become a chaplain, reinforces the method of Action—Reflection—Action. When you go through an experience, you learn. Upon reflection and understanding, you are better able to apply that learning the next time a similar experience happens. I'd say the same for the fruit of the Spirit. When something happens, we have the chance to contemplate: Did I show love, joy, peace, patience, kindness, goodness, faithfulness, gentleness, and self-control? And how could I better reflect God next time?

Let Us Pray

Holy Spirit, let me show love and joy today.
Spirit of the Lord, help me show peace and patience today.

Spirit of God, help me show kindness and goodness today.

Spirit, help me show faithfulness, gentleness, and self-control today.

And forgive me and help me grow when I do not. Amen.

Reflection Questions

1. Which example story from this chapter resonated with you?

2. Which fruit of the Spirit do you show regularly? Which is more difficult?

3. Look at the description for forbearance. Can you give an example of where you've seen this fruit?

4. When you think of the fruit of the Sprit, which actual fruits come to your mind?

5. How entangled are you with Holy Spirit? How have you grown?

CHAPTER

7

OVERFLOWING WITH PURPOSE AND POWER

*May the God of hope fill you with all joy and peace
as you trust in him, so that you may overflow
with hope by the power of the Holy Spirit.*

—Romans 15:13, NIV

As I was starting this last chapter of the book, I felt called to a spiritual retreat. I had the desire for the Holy Spirit to guide me in what yet needed to be said. My fear was that this might be the shortest chapter in the history of book writing.

In the northeast corner of our state is a retreat center that formerly was a monastery. I had gone to the abbey for a focusing and writing sanctuary years ago and felt that this was the place where I needed to return. This particular abbey's purpose was to establish missions and schools (both of which resonate with my life), largely on Native American reservations. As the numbers of monks dwindled, the abbey closed as a monastery and has now been converted to a retreat center.

In preparation for the retreat, I prayed that the Holy Spirit would make it known what I should write, that it wouldn't be my ideas alone. I asked a small group of people to pray for my time. I also hesitated to do any writing or planning until I was at the center. When I arrived, it was a beautiful night. The stars were bright and gorgeous, and I sat outside in God's splendor. Then I settled in my room to read Scripture and *The Rule of Saint Benedict,* which was on the bedside stand, until I fell asleep.

The next morning, I went for a walk. It was crisp; okay, it was downright cold. The abbey is on the top of rolling hills, and if you know anything about the Dakotas, there's always wind. Always. Okay, Holy Spirit. I know about your mighty winds; I feel them on my face. I'm ready to listen for your gentle whispers.

Two small lakes are near the center, the Lower Lake and the Upper Lake. The walk around the Lower Lake is a well-groomed trail, and with fall colors on the leaves and a light dusting of snow, it was a beautiful stroll. The trail around the Upper Lake is primitive. At times, the path is hard to determine; it closely follows the edge of the lake; there are rocks on the path, and there are tree branches hanging low. I was carefully stepping my way around the lake and it came to me, *"Look up. Look up and see what you're missing."* Three whitetail deer gave me a glance and pranced off. A blue jay overhead. About twenty turkeys foraging. A sunrise cracking the horizon, shining through the trees, and reflecting on the lake. How often are we so consumed with our own feet, our own rocky path, that we miss the beauty right before us? Look up.

When I finished my walk, it came to me, *"Go to the chapel."* At the abbey there is a sandstone chapel lined with stained glass windows. I thought back to the mass I attended with the monks years ago; the prayers, songs, and words delivered in measured, paced, and holy tones. This morning, the sun cast intricate shadows along the walls. It was a kaleidoscope of color. And I felt compelled to consider, "How am I reflecting the light of God, Jesus, and the Holy Spirit?"

Throughout my retreat walks, prayer, and gentle moments, there were four themes that kept repeating themselves: make it simple, don't underestimate My power, look up, reflect the light.

Make It Simple

It became clear to me why I was called to this place. The life in a monastery is simple living. Monks live their lives in simplicity.

More than fifteen hundred years ago, Benedict of Nursia wrote guidelines, *The Rule of St. Benedict,* about how a monastery should function. My favorite one is: "They sleep fully clothed and girded with belts or cords; but they should remove their knives, lest they accidentally cut themselves in their sleep." Safety first!

Guidance on how to live is paramount to monastic life. The hallmarks and commitments to this life are outlined in "rules" of unhesitating obedience, restraint of speech, tools for good works, and twelve individual steps to reach humility.

Be obedient. When Jesus ascended, he sent the Holy Spirit to dwell within us. Jesus gave us an incredible gift, and our role is to be obedient—unhesitatingly obedient.

> If the Spirit of him who raised Jesus from the dead dwells in you, he who raised Christ Jesus from the dead will also give life to your mortal bodies through his Spirit who dwells in you. (Romans 8:11)

We don't need to know everything today; it will be revealed to us. Speak less and listen more for the Holy Spirit. Restrain *our* speech so the Spirit can speak.

> "I have much more to say to you, more than you can now bear. But when he, the Spirit of truth, comes, he will guide you into all the truth. He will not speak on his own; he

will speak only what he hears, and he will tell you what is
yet to come." (John 16:12-13, NIV)

Live humbly and do good works. We have received gifts of the
Holy Spirit; use them. We have the fruit of the Spirit as evidence of our
Christlikeness. The Holy Spirit convicts us to take action—to make that
call, to send a message, to help someone we don't know, to help someone we do know, to make a difference by responding, to accept help
when needed, to give help when needed, to live a life worthy of Christ.

> But be doers of the word, and not hearers only, deceiving
> yourselves. (James 1:22, NKJV)

> Clothe yourselves, all of you, with humility toward one
> another, for "God opposes the proud but gives grace to
> the humble." (1 Peter 5:5)

Don't Underestimate My Power

A bell tower chimes on each quarter hour. Back in the day, it called
the monks to prayer. At first, the bells startled me; it's so quiet here,
the bells were an unexpected interruption to the peace. But as my
time wore on, the chimes just became part of the day.

As a relative newcomer to the Holy Spirit, the one thing that surprised me initially was that the Holy Spirit is a person. My brother was
reading a draft of my early chapters, and he said, "The greatest challenge I had was fully accepting the premise that the Spirit is a person."

If this was a revelation to you, startled you, my hope is that as
the book has continued it has become part of your belief. The Holy
Spirit has attributes of a person, acts like a person, and is treated like
a person in the Scriptures. Not a limited, fallible person like us, but
a divine person. The Holy Spirit is a who, not a what. If this is still

ringing bells for you, and you want to learn more, check out Jason Byassee's book *Trinity: The God We Don't Know* (Nashville: Abingdon Press, 2015). If you really want to dig in, check out Elmer M. Colyer's book, *The Trinitarian Dimension of John Wesley's Theology* (New Room Books, 2019).

I include this because when we think of the Spirit as a person, it's completely different. We can be held accountable; the Spirit is someone whom we can relate to, share with, and focus on. If we see the Holy Spirit only as a nebulous concept or feeling, it's easier to push the Holy Spirit aside as a something instead of a someone.

The Holy Spirit dwells within us; now release the power! My prayer is that the *Listen—Hear—Respond* sections, and other stories from real people, encouraged but also challenged you. Through the power of the Holy Spirit, we can discover awe, change direction, be a messenger, rescue others, work through tragedies, be the right person at the right time, confirm our direction, learn to trust, receive gifts, heal through prayer, enact miracles, declare goodness, be called into mission, bring joy, be at peace, make life changes, restore relationships, bring kindness, reconcile families, and help others, among so many other things.

> For those who are led by the Spirit of God are the children of God. (Romans 8:14, NIV)

Listen—Hear—Respond

We met Shirley and Joe Edgerton in 2008 when they were missionaries on the island of La Gonâve, Haiti. They introduced us to William, whom we talked about earlier in this book, an orphan who had a dream of becoming a doctor. In 2010, William and I were with a medical team on La Gonâve during the massive earthquake, but

Shirley and Joe were in Port-au-Prince and had a much more dramatic experience. In addition to providing care for many, they were responsible for identifying and transporting the body of Rev. Sam Dixon, then director of the United Methodist Committee on Relief, back to the United States.

Shirley and Joe exemplify listening, hearing, and responding to the Holy Spirit. Their story of grace in the midst of tragedy could fill this entire book. Here are Shirley's reflections days after the 2010 Haiti earthquake.

We have washed the smell of decaying bodies from our clothing and sit before a wooden wick candle burning on a hundred-year-old coffee table in our hundred-year-old bungalow, listening to an acoustic guitar playing a mournful tune, and try not to think of the last week of our lives. A week of terror, death, and destruction bracketed by spontaneous praise to a God who secured the night with prayer and chants to beg God's protection and preparation for a new day of uncertainty.

Days ago, we shared the terror of an earthquake with our Haitian friends as the world collapsed in a cloud of dirt, broken water lines, and crushed bodies. Homes of millions avalanched down mountainsides as an already hopeless lifestyle became one of confusion, death, and chaos. A culture developing the rudiments of new technology was reduced, once again, to isolation from communication, hunters of food rotting in smashed markets, and water under layers of dirt and debris. Clinging together, we helped dig through tons of collapsed rock and concrete to find nine-year-old babies and ninety-year-old angels.

At the time of the earthquake, Joe and I were meeting with a student beside the pool. The chair went out from under me, and I tried to pull the student down as Joe "danced" away from us! I looked back at the swimming pool and took note of how tsunamis form! Gallons of water were bouncing out of the pool as all the walls around the perimeter were shattering and the large building to the north was being rearranged. The Guest House was sliding along with the concrete patio about a foot back and forth. The approximate thirty seconds of violence seemed like an hour.

Following the quake several very old, frail ladies were trapped when the cement roof and walls of a big house along the alley collapsed. We eventually extracted one lady and managed to carry her to a tap-tap (Haiti taxi) parked outside our gate. She had a head injury and had suffered a blow to the chest and face. She survived until the next afternoon. The next day we found another lady trapped much higher in the rubble and eventually we got her out . . . unhurt. . . . She is an angel and encourages us all from a padded chair under the tarp. There is still one lady (the three were sisters) still in there somewhere, but we have heard no sounds from her and have no way to reach that high.

With repeated trips to the mountain, we eventually located Sam's body and began the process to bring him home to his grieving wife. Others there weren't interested in helping us sort through body bags to find him, they had their own loved ones to find. Now I sit, having searched and secured the body of a lost colleague to his loved ones, and I weep with God because of a nation in a palpable pain.

Once I sat at the bedside of my comatose son, whose skull was broken, and my heart hurt so bad—I could not breathe; I could not pray; I could not swallow. This night, I cannot swallow. I can only turn off National Public Radio and give thanks we have no TV to subject me to the negative assessments of a broken, desperate people and those attempting to hold together a gaping hole leaking out the life of a nation. Tonight, I allow myself to sit by the bedside of my Haitian friends who fight desperately to locate the lost and live, themselves, through another night. Tonight, I allow myself to grieve. There is nothing more I can do this night.

I am safe and warm in a cold world. I have the face of a young man before me, asking "Madame, I am hungry and have no money, won't you give me one dollar?" I tell him I have not enough dollars for all who stand with him, uncertain and hungry. He asks, "What will we do? Will the water swallow us?" I tell him, I do not know what he can do but the water is not his enemy. I tell him, "Help will come." I will keep his face in my heart and tell my people his friends are hungry. I ache to embrace this almost child with a scarred face but take him by the shoulders, and I cannot swallow. He thanks me, and I leave with my dead friend.

There is a time for everything, the Scriptures say. Tonight is my time to cry. Tomorrow there is much work to do: phone calls to make; emails to send; prayers to pray; stories to tell; funds to raise; plans to make; money to send; buried bodies to find; bodies to bury; questions to answer; answers to seek; and worrying to do.

We learned in two years of living on La Gonâve, you can take nothing for granted in Haiti, other than the presence of God. Most assuredly the presence of God is in this place. May the thousands who have perished be at peace in the embrace of God, and those whose lives are broken, be healed by the grace of God.

Look Up

Look up and see the world beyond our feet. People need us, they need God, they need Jesus, they need the Holy Spirit. Where is it that you can listen, hear, and then respond?

Life in a monastery can be summed up in these three things: solitude, prayer, and working for others. With our cell phones in hand, we are constantly distracted. That email or Instagram post *has to* happen now. Or maybe the earth won't come crashing in if we turn off our technology. Wesley called prayer the chief means of grace, and it's our way to concentrate on God, others, and ourselves. Yes, your family needs you to bring in an income. Yes, your family needs you to take out the trash and wash the dishes. Yes, your family and others need your time and attention.

Spend more moments appreciating the goodness of God. Take that walk. Ride your bike. Take that trip you've been putting off. Lie under a canopy of stars. Play a game with your grandchild. Bring your spouse to that special restaurant. Look at a flower up close. Stoke the firepit. Let the power of God's beauty enfold you as you foster your appreciation of the simple.

Pray about and understand your gifts. Then release them like powerful winds to accomplish the purposes of the Holy Spirit.

Reflect the Light

When we look in the mirror, do we see love, joy, peace, patience, kindness, goodness, faithfulness, gentleness, and self-control? When someone looks at us, do they see love, joy, peace, patience, kindness, goodness, faithfulness, gentleness, and self-control?

Pray about and understand how you show fruit, how you reflect the light of Christ. Then be ready to hear the silent whispers, and unleash the power of the Holy Spirit.

> Gracious and Holy Father,
> Please give me:
> intellect to understand you,
> reason to discern you,
> diligence to seek you,
> wisdom to find you,
> a spirit to know you,
> a heart to meditate upon you,
> ears to hear you,
> eyes to see you,
> a tongue to proclaim you,
> a way of life pleasing to you,
> patience to wait for you
> and perseverance to look for you.
> Grant me a perfect end,
> your holy presence,
> a blessed resurrection
> and life everlasting.
> —St. Benedict of Nursia (ca. 480–547)

BIBLIOGRAPHY

Barclay, William. *Daily Study Bible Commentaries*. Louisville: Westminster John Knox Press, 1955.

Bevere, John, and Addison Bevere. *The Holy Spirit: An Introduction*. Palmer Lake, CO: Messenger International, 2013.

Chan, Francis, and Danae Yankoski. *Forgotten God: Reversing Our Tragic Neglect of the Holy Spirit*. Colorado Springs: David C. Cook, 2009.

Dragos, Andrew. "How John Wesley's Means of Grace Should Impact our Christian Witness." Seedbed, May 29, 2012. https://www.seedbed.com/how -john-wesleys-means-of-grace-should-impact-our-christian-witness/.

Fry, Timothy, ed. *RB 1980: The Rule of St. Benedict in English*. Collegeville, MN: Liturgical Press, 1982.

Graham, Billy. *The Holy Spirit: Activating God's Power in Your Life*. Nashville: Thomas Nelson, 2000.

Howard, Cathy. "What Are the Fruit of the Holy Spirit?" Crosswalk.com, March 26, 2018. https://www.crosswalk.com/faith/spiritual-life/what-are -the-fruit-of-the-spirit.html.

Jackson, Thomas, ed. *The Works of John Wesley*. 14 vols. Grand Rapids: Baker Book House, 1984.

Keating, Thomas. *Fruits and Gifts of the Spirit*. New York: Lantern Books, 2007.

Koulianos, Michael. *Holy Spirit: The One Who Makes Jesus Real*. Shippensburg, PA: Destiny Image, 2017.

Lawson, Arvest. *The Holy Spirit in John Wesley's Theology*. Kearney, NE: Morris, 1999.

Morris, Robert. *The God I Never Knew: How Real Friendship with the Holy Spirit Can Change Your Life*. Colorado Springs: WaterBrook, 2013.

Nerburn, Kent. *The Wolf at Twilight: An Indian Elder's Journey Through a Land of Ghosts and Shadows*. Novata, CA: New World Library, 2009.

Norris, Kathleen. *Dakota: A Spiritual Geography.* New York: Mariner Books, 2001.

Noyes, Penny. "What Are the Fruits of the Spirit?" Christianity.com, February 26, 2019. https://www.christianity.com/wiki/holy-spirit/what-are -the-fruits-of-the-spirit.html.

Ponsonby, Simon. *God Inside Out: An In-Depth Study of the Holy Spirit.* Edinburgh: Muddy Pearl, 2015.

Stanley, Charles F. *Living in the Power of the Holy Spirit.* Nashville: Thomas Nelson, 2005.

Stewart, Don. Is the Holy Spirit a Person? BlueLetterBible.org. https://www .blueletterbible.org/Comm/stewart_don/faq/the-identity-of-the-holy-spirit /05-is-the-holy-spirit-a-person.cfm.

Taylor, Justin. "How Do We Know the Holy Spirit Is a Person?" TheGospelCoalition.org, December 12, 2013. https://www.thegospelcoalition.org/blogs /justin-taylor/how-do-we-know-the-holy-spirit-is-a-person/.

Tozer, A. W. *How to Be Filled with the Holy Spirit.* Mansfield Center, CT: Martino, 2017.

Wesley, John. *Holy Spirit and Power.* Edited by Clare Weakley. Newberry, FL: Bridge-Logos, 2003.

NOTES

1 Simon Ponsonby, in an endorsement of Francis Chan, *Forgotten God: Reversing Our Tragic Neglect of the Holy Spirit* (Colorado Springs: David C. Cook, 2009), front matter.

2 A. W. Tozer, *How to Be Filled with the Holy Spirit* (n.p.: GLH, 2017), chap. 1.

3 John Bevere, with Addison Bevere, *The Holy Spirit: An Introduction* (Palmer Lake, CO: Messenger International, 2013), n.p.

4 Francesca Battistelli, "Holy Spirit," by Katie Torwalt and Bryan Wilson, in *If We're Honest*, Word, Fervent, 2014, studio album.

5 Robert Morris, *The God I Never Knew: How Friendship with the Holy Spirit Can Change Your Life* (Colorado Springs: Waterbrook, 2011), 29.

6 William Barclay, *The Acts of the Disciples*, reissue ed. (Louisville: Westminster John Knox Press, 2017), first published in 1953 as *The Daily Study Bible: The Acts of the Apostles*.

7 Barclay, n.p.

8 Steven J. Cole, "Lesson 5: The Sermon that Launched the Church," Bible.org, 2000, https://bible.org/seriespage/lesson-5-sermon-launched-church-acts-214-41.

9 Bevere, *The Holy Spirit*, n.p.

10 Francis Chan, *Forgotten God: Reversing Our Tragic Neglect of the Holy Spirit* (Colorado Springs: David C. Cook, 2009), 37.

11 Charles F. Stanley, *Living in the Power of the Holy Spirit* (Nashville: Thomas Nelson, 2005), 22.

12 Stanley, 33.

13 Stanley, 33.

14 Billy Graham, *The Holy Spirit: Activating God's Power in Your Life*, reissue ed. (Nashville: Thomas Nelson, 2000), 92.

15 Stanley, *Living in the Power of the Holy Spirit*, 51.

16 Tozer, *How to Be Filled with the Holy Spirit*, n.p.

17 Stanley, *Living in the Power of the Holy Spirit*, 60.

18 Stanley, 45.

19 Tozer, *How to Be Filled with the Holy Spirit*, n.p.

20 Arvest N. Lawson, *The Holy Spirit in John Wesley's Theology* (Kearney, NE: Morris, 1999), 21.

21 Chris Ritter, "Seven Ways John Wesley Preached About the Holy Spirit," People Need Jesus, May 30, 2017, https://peopleneedjesus.net/2017/05/30/seven-ways-john -wesley-preached-about-the-holy-spirit/.

22 *The Journal of John Wesley*, vol. 1 (London: Charles H. Kelly, 1903), 54.

23 John Wesley, *The Holy Spirit and Power*, ed. Clare Weakley (Alachua, FL: Bridge-Logos, 2003), 15.

24 Wesley, 16.

25 Wesley, 18.

26 Wesley, 18.

27 Wesley, 18.

28 Wesley, 23.

29 Wesley, 23.

30 Wesley, 26.

31 Wesley, 26–27.

32 Lawson, *The Holy Spirit in John Wesley's Theology*, 26.

33 Lawson, 27.

34 John Wesley, "A Letter to the Reverend Dr. Conyers Middleton," in *The Works of John Wesley*, vol. 8, *Letters, Essays, Dialogs and Addresses* (Grand Rapids: Zondervan, 1872), 68.

35 Lawson, *The Holy Spirit in John Wesley's Theology*, 30.

36 Bruce L. Blumer, *Simply Grace: Everyday Glimpses of God* (Wesley's Foundery Books, 2019).

37 Mark K. Olson, "John Wesley's Doctrine of the Holy Spirit," WesleyScholar.com, September 14, 2019, https://wesleyscholar.com/john-wesleys-doctrine-of-the-holy-spirit/.

38 Olson.

39 Olson.

40 Steve Harper, *Devotional Life in the Wesleyan Tradition* (Nashville: Upper Room Books, 1983), 19.

41 E. Stanley Jones, "What Is Prayer?" in E. Stanley Jones Foundation, *How to Pray* newsletter, 2013, http://www.estanleyjonesfoundation.com/wp-content/uploads/2014/01 /2013-How-to-Pray-Newsletter.pdf, 2.

42 Charles Spurgeon, *Morning and Evening*, upd. ed. (New Kensington, PA: Whitaker House, 2001), January 14 evening, 41.

43 Kent Nerburn, *The Wolf at Twilight: An Indian Elder's Journey through a Land of Ghosts and Shadows* (Novata, CA: New World Library, 2009), n.p.

44 Lawson, *The Holy Spirit in John Wesley's Theology*, 46.

45 Emanuel Cleaver, *What Is the Bible and Who Is It For? A Book for Beginners, Skeptics, and Seekers* (Nashville: GBHEM, 2020).

46 John Wesley, "The Duty of Constant Communion," in Kenneth J. Collins and Jason E. Vickers, eds., *The Sermons of Wesley: A Collection for the Christian Journey* (Nashville: Abingdon, 2013), 84–93.

47 Emily Snell, "Means of Grace: Fasting and Holy Communion," Resource UMC, accessed May 12, 2021, https://www.resourceumc.org/en/content/means-of-grace-fasting-and-holy-communion.

48 Steve Manskar, "Fasting: The most neglected means of grace," ResourceUMC, February 18, 2015, https://www.resourceumc.org/en/content/fasting-the-most-neglected-means-of-grace.

49 Danny Gokey, featuring Michael W. Smith, "Love God, Love People," by Jeff Sojka, Colby Wedgeworth, Ben Glover, Danny Gokey, and Riley Clemmons, in *Haven't Seen It Yet*, Capitol CMG, 2019, album.

50 Lester Sumrall, *The Gifts and Ministries of the Holy Spirit* (New Kensington, PA: Whitaker House, 2005), chap. 1.

51 Lawson, *The Holy Spirit in John Wesley's Theology*, 22.

52 See Sumrall, *The Gifts and Ministries of the Holy Spirit*, chaps. 6–9.

53 Sumrall, n.p.

54 "Spiritual Gifts: Wisdom," The United Methodist Church website, September 9, 2019, https://cdnsc.umc.org/en/content/spiritual-gifts-wisdom.

55 See Michael Koulianos, *Holy Spirit: The One Who Makes Jesus Real* (Shippensburg, PA: Destiny Image, 2017).

56 "Spiritual Gift of Miracles," Spiritual Gifts Test, accessed May 12, 2021, https://spiritualgiftstest.com/spiritual-gift-miracles/.

57 Brannon Deibert, "What Are the Gifts of the Holy Spirit? Scripture Quotes and Meaning," Christianity.com, February 14, 2019, https://www.christianity.com/god/holy-spirit/what-are-the-seven-gifts-of-the-holy-spirit-scripture-meaning.html.

58 "Spiritual Gifts: Prophecy," The United Methodist Church website, September 9, 2019, https://www.umc.org/en/content/spiritual-gifts-prophecy.

59 Lawson, *The Holy Spirit in John Wesley's Theology*, n.p.

60 Lawson, n.p.

61 Al Carmines, "Many Gifts, One Spirit," *The United Methodist Hymnal*, 114.

62 Graham, *The Holy Spirit*, 239, italics in original.

63 Lawson, *The Holy Spirit in John Wesley's Theology*, 31.

64 See Tristen Coffee, "If the Fruit of the Spirit Were Actual Fruit," *Odyssey* (blog), March 15, 2016, https://www.theodysseyonline.com/fruits-spirit-actual-fruits.

65 William Barclay, *Daily Bible Study Commentaries* (Louisville: Westminster John Knox Press, 1955), n.p.

66 Mother Teresa, *No Greater Love* (Novato, CA: New World Library, 2010), 20.

67 Carrie Underwood, "Jesus, Take the Wheel," by Brett James, Hillary Lindsey, and Gordie Sampson, in *Some Hearts*, Arista, 2005, album.